RADIATE

CHANGE YOUR FREQUENCY
CHANGE YOUR LIFE

ROCHEL RITTGERS

Radiate: Change Your Frequency, Change Your Life

All Rights Reserved

ISBN:
Paperback - 978-1-954759-39-8
Hardcover - 978-1-954759-40-4
EBook - 978-1-954759-38-1

Cranberry Press Publish

When we understand that frequency is everything, our world will shift and bring forth a new horizon. In this timeless work, the fundamentals of life are easily digestible from a frequency standpoint, with the most important work of releasing stored low frequency emotions as a focus.

"Radiate" is a treasury of insights into a modern look at frequency. It is a wonderful book to heal emotional density, release pain, and forge a path to love. Rittgers incorporates ancient ways with present-day systems anyone can use to raise their spiritual frequency and alleviate personal suffering.

Blessings of gratitude and light,

Rochel

Table Of Contents

Introduction

What is your frequency? Are you on the wavelength that will provide you the most health and happiness? What about your environment — are the frequencies of your home, your neighborhood, or even your workplace good for your overall well-being?

Some people are sensitive to frequencies. Others are less so. But frequency affects all of us. Whether it's a sense of agitation, or a sense that something's not quite right, whether it's emotional instability or elation, most of how we feel and live can be attributed to frequency.

Becoming aware of the power of frequency means you can harness frequency to move ahead. You can unlock stored emotions and heal yourself.

This book explores frequency and more — it looks at all aspects of your health and environment, from eating and sleeping to breathing and thinking. I deal with the emotional state you might be in due to your past experiences or traumas, or your present situation or physical environment. This book is based on my experience as a licensed sports medicine professional, and then as a Qigong master. Over the years, I have realized that spirituality can be combined with my love of caring for the human body. I share my passion with you. I am an energy Master, a breakthrough strategist and CEO of Infinite Living, helping people who are stuck in business and in life to uncover the seed that is holding them back so they can THRIVE and move forward in their life, in the most empowered and vibrant way.

In each chapter, you'll find ideas that I illustrate through personal stories. I then provide you with steps and methods that will help you put into action the concepts I cover. Throughout this book, I urge you to take time to step back, breathe and meditate to better comprehend where you are, where you're going and how you can handle the traumas of your past to create a peaceful and engaging life. I hope that you will turn to this book again and again, and find some new aspects of frequency or state of being that you can address, with solutions that you can apply to your everyday life and your spiritual path.

Chapter 1

Tune to the Life Frequency You Want

"If you want to find the secrets of the universe, think in terms of energy, frequency and vibration," said Nikola Tesla, the noted inventor. Another genius, Albert Einstein, said, "Concerning matter, we have been all wrong. What we have called matter is energy, whose vibration has been so lowered as to be imperceptible to the senses. There is no matter."

What it comes down to is frequency. It's everywhere, and we often don't pay attention to it and how it affects us.

But once you get a sense of frequency, and once you become aware of how to attract it, use it, raise it or lower it, your life will change for the better.

Becoming aware of the power of frequency means you can harness frequency to move ahead. You can unlock stored emotions and heal yourself.

Here you'll find different approaches to frequency and how it affects you. You will find stories from my life and from the people I have encountered. I will also provide you with steps and methods to put these ideas into practice.

Your world is a blur of vibration. Tune your dial to any frequency to achieve the life you desire. You get to choose the frequency of your life. Dial up for joy, dial down for discomfort.

I'll share a story about the Schumann Resonance, what it is, and how it plays a role in choosing your frequency. I will also give you steps to take you through these:

- Employing a daily Qigong practice

- Initiating a daily meditation practice

- Adding yoga or some other active movement into your day

- Practicing techniques for being present

Since 2012, we have become more aware of the resonance of the planet that has been affecting us in significant ways. The resonance derives from the collective frequency of all electromagnetic activity of the planet and the sun — lightning, volcanoes, earthquakes, solar flares, coronal mass ejections, as well as human emotions.

The Schumann resonances are a set of spectrum peaks in the extremely low frequency portion of the Earth's electromagnetic field spectrum. Schumann resonances are global electromagnetic resonances, generated and excited by lightning discharges in the cavity formed by the Earth's surface and the ionosphere.

This measures a spectrum of peaks in the Earth's collective electromagnetic field. Our planet's normal frequency resonates at 7.83 Hertz. The surprising change is that there are amplitude spikes occurring that haven't been prevalent before. Since 2012, the amplitude spikes have been progressively getting higher and higher. The average resonance remains the same at 7.83, but the elevated spikes can be continuous over the course of hours and even days.

Those spikes affect us in powerful ways. They impact our physiology by being absorbed by our brain systems and altering the serotonin/melatonin balance. Serotonin is a naturally occurring substance that functions as a neurotransmitter to carry signals between nerve cells throughout our bodies. It helps with mood regulation, memory, promotes healthy digestion, and produces melatonin, which is responsible for your sleep cycle.

Over the last eleven years, I have consciously allowed these frequencies to flow through my body, breaking loose old, stored emotions, and bringing them to the surface to be healed. I used to have layers and layers of stored emotional density. This resulted in my becoming anxious, having a low-grade level of depression, getting angry too easily, and generally just not being all that happy.

I'm normally a relatively happy person, but I was feeling stressed and that I needed to protect myself in some ways. And I had been sitting back, somewhat disengaged from living my life fully. As each of the emotional layers has been jostled, stored emotions from past emotional trauma have arisen. I have been able to embrace even those really dark parts of me that have been hidden for so long and release them.

Raising your vibrational frequency will correspondingly raise the level of your experiences. If you are seeking to improve your life's experiences, you may be interested in knowing how to navigate this world of frequency in order to support a comfortable physical and emotional life.

Steps and Methods

There are many possible methods to achieve this and the following are ways I have used, and you can successfully use them for yourself, also.

Practice Qigong Daily. Qigong exercises use body movement techniques intended to assist in the flow of energy around you and through you, and they are effective at balancing your energy and bringing you into a state of peace. Complete relaxation of all areas of the body is the physical state that is most conducive to being open to shifting energy flow. I have studied the simple yet powerful Spring Forest Qigong for 16 years, and I recommend the online Spring Forest Qigong YouTube channel. There are many free Qigong exercise videos there to follow. Use these in your daily routine.

Initiate a meditation practice. A meditation practice is the fastest and most effective way to elevate your frequency. One of my favorites is a technique that focuses on using your breath. You use your intention to move your breath through the main energy points in your body:

- Start by finding a quiet place where you won't be disturbed.

- Sit or lie down with your spine straight and your ears in alignment with your shoulders and hips.

- On inhaling, imagine your breath coming in through the bottom of your feet and traveling up your body to the top of your head.

- Then on exhaling, the breath travels from the top of your head, down your whole body, and out the bottom of your feet. Repeat this several times.

- With each repeat, visualize in your mind the path opening more and more, and the flow of energy getting easier and easier.

Practice Yoga Regularly. For more than 4,000 years, yoga has been an effective tool to improve your health, and your frequency. Any type of gentle to moderate movement helps to enhance the positive flow of energy through you. Yoga is readily available in most communities these days, and online.

Practice techniques for being present. What is being present? Because our lives are filled with so many things that can distract us, our physical body is often in one place, and our mind is in another. Our mind is wandering into our to-do lists, or a conversation we had an hour ago, or what we are having to eat for dinner, or an infinite number of other places. The act of being present means our body and our mind are engaged in the same place on the same task at the same time. When we are present, our mind is not able to conjure up negative thoughts that can further block our energy.

There are many ways to practice being present. Here are a few ideas:

- Take a 4-by-6-inch white index card and draw a ½-inch black circle in the middle of that card. Fill in the circle so it is a ½-inch black dot. Hang the card on a wall with the dot at eye level. Stand about a foot away from the card and stare at the dot. How long can you stare at the dot before you blink? Practice this daily to enhance your level of focus and presence.

- Be present to the sound vibrations in your environment by sitting and listening. Listen to all the sounds around you without attaching an opinion or emotion to them. For each sound, allow the vibrations of that sound to resonate through you, perhaps even sensing them in your tissues.

- You can also be present to color. Sit in a quiet place and look at a flower, deeply. How long can you keep your mind centered on that flower? Look deeply into the color variations in that flower. How many nuances of color can you see in that flower? How many things can you learn about that flower by studying it deeply?

Through practicing these techniques and releasing many layers of stored density, my life has become a brilliant journey, filled with high frequency people, high-frequency experiences, and frequent, unapologetic outbursts of unbridled joy. This is what I want for you.

You Are the Microcosm of the Macrocosm

Are you a clanging bell, just making noise to be heard? You are the microcosm, and the universe is the macrocosm. Everything about each of us as individuals is a microcosm representing our own personal frequency, and also representing the grander macrocosm of the world around us. What are you reflecting out into the world?

Here we'll explore our influence on ourselves, on our environment, and on the planet as a whole. We will discuss how stored emotions from past trauma have an unfavorable impact on our lives and the world around us, and how stored digestive toxins can also have a similar effect.

Have you ever been around people who like to hear themselves talk? They fill up silence with idle chatter. When we put any energy out into the Universe, whether it be a thought, an emotion, an internal trauma, or a sound, it continues to reverberate throughout the Universe, infinitely. When we can control the number of thoughts and the amount of words that go out into the Universe, we can control the frequency we are putting out.

Do we want to fill our silence with noise that can translate into low-frequency, energy-sapping, health-depleting noise? Or do we want to fill our silence with meaning that translates into frequency-elevating, energy-filling, health-enhancing sound? I encourage you to be conscious about the vibrations you send out in the form of words, thoughts, deep intentions, and inner storage related to past trauma, stored emotions, and digestive toxins.

Steps and Methods

The following areas of our lives have the greatest impact on the frequency we hold.

Emotions Stored from Inner Trauma. Emotions resulting from inner, unreleased trauma have a major influence on the frequency you resonate out into the environment. Everyone comes into this human experience with lessons to learn. We learn them through difficult experiences in our lives, especially in our earliest years. Out of these traumatic experiences, we create shadow beliefs about who we are — I am unlovable, I am worthless, I am stupid, I am not enough, I don't matter, and many more.

Shadow beliefs set the stage for who we believe we are, and how we experience the world around us. We store the emotions associated with those traumas in our bodies, which affects the frequency of the thoughts we think, the decisions we make, the relationships we have, the health of our bodies, and even our employment. They dictate the outcomes in all areas of our lives. As we release those stored emotions, the frequency of our body elevates, and therefore the frequency of our experiences elevate, our life experiences begin to shift to higher frequency, personal satisfaction results, and inner peace is experienced.

Digestive toxins. Digestive toxins held inside your body also create a density affecting your frequency. If we all grew our own fruits and veggies and made our own food, we would likely not hold so many digestive toxins inside our bodies. Since most of us don't grow or produce our own food, we rely on the food industry to provide us with the sustenance we use to feed our bodies. We are subject to indigestible ingredients put into our food for preser-vation, stability, taste, etc. If we eat a lot of processed foods, our body's frequency becomes that of processed foods, and so our body desires more processed food.

The same holds true with fresh foods. But the food industry also adds chemicals to processed food that makes it addictive. Fresh foods do not have that same addictive capacity. Toxins cause us to make lower frequency food choices, which add more toxins to our bodies.

The Frequency of Your Thoughts. What are low-frequency thoughts? Thinking poorly of ourselves, or judging others. Thoughts of rejection, loneliness, or burden. Thoughts of blame, shame, or unhappiness. Our low-frequency thoughts reflect the shadow beliefs we believe about ourselves, from traumas we have experienced.

The Frequency of the Words We Speak. Our words are a projection of the thoughts we hold inside. When people hold low frequency inside, the words that roll from their tongue will reflect their internal frequency.

When you do your inner work, detoxify your body and become intentional with your thoughts and words, your entire life will improve. This has been true in my life, and it will work for you as well. Each of these areas works hand-in-hand. Removing toxins from your digestion elevates the frequency of your thoughts. When you elevate your thoughts, your words automatically improve. The same is true with doing your inner work to release the stored emotional trauma. When you peel away the layers of trauma in your heart and mind, your belief in yourself elevates, which improves your thought loop that plays in your head, and that improves the quality of words that flow from your lips to the ears of your listeners. We are magnificent creatures, interconnected in every way!

Frequency: The Supreme Ruler

Frequency is the foundation of everything in our lives. We can use it to our highest benefit or we can ignore it. If we ignore it, it still affects us at the level of our personal-default frequency.

Here we will explore the effects of frequency, and share a story about how Tibetan monks have been using the benefits of frequency for thousands of years.

I will also guide you through recognizing and polishing the music of your frequency:

- Listen deeply to the frequency of a piece of music you enjoy.

- Feel into the frequency of that music within your body.

- Identify where you feel it, and how it feels.

- Repeat the process with a piece of music you don't like.

- Now do the experiment with a well-established chant.

When you engage in these practices, you will not only know the value, but you will feel the value of consciously directing your frequency so you can live the most dynamic, purpose-driven life that is possible for you.

The Power of 'Om'

When I first started chanting, I thought it felt awkward. I began with "om," because it was easy to remember, and it seemed less distracting than trying to recite a phrase. Even so, it felt new and odd. Through continued practice, I began to realize there was a sensation in my body. My whole body responded to this chant. I could feel the vibration in different locations in my body.

When I used other chants, the locations of the vibrations in my body changed. The locations seemed to depend on the note, the word, and the octave being chanted. My body also seemed to resonate with more intensity, depending on the amount of spiritual history behind the chant. Chants even send vibrational frequencies into our auric and etheric bodies, the area beyond our physical bodies.

The meaning in each chant adds to its power, too. We receive these as healing prayers. They also transmit into the Universe as healing prayers. Because Masters have used ancient chants for centuries, these chants hold an even higher frequency. I encourage you to step into the world of chanting to experience inner and outer shifts in your life.

Steps and Methods

Here are some ways that can help you to fully experience frequency for yourself:

Listen deeply to the frequency of a piece of music you enjoy. Choose a piece of music that makes you happy every time you hear it. Listen with your heart. Listen with your whole being. Listen and experience what happens all through you.

Feel into the frequency of that music within your body. Listen with your whole body. Hear it with your ears, and also with your body. Experience the depth and quality of that vibration from the perspective of every one of your senses.

Identify where and how you feel the music. Feel where the music vibrates inside of you. Identify the location. If it's your liver, does a memory bubble up? If your heart, what is that message? Is an emotion attached to it? Perhaps you have been distracted from paying attention to it in the past because you were unaware of the possibilities it could teach you.

Repeat the process with a piece of music that you don't like. After doing the experiment with a piece of music you love, repeat the process with a piece of music that you don't like. Are there differences in the way it resonates, through and all around your body. If a piece of music affects every aspect of you in either a positive or a negative way, does it give you reason to choose differently when choosing your music?

Now do the experiment with a well-established chant. After experiencing this process with enjoyable music and with music you don't enjoy, do the experiment with a well-established chant. The easiest and most powerful chant that I talked about before is the word Om. This is said to resonate at the frequency of the vibration of all of creation. It is said to help you connect with your true essence.

Are You a Relevant Resonator?

Your frequency matters. The energy you radiate impacts you and your environment.

Here we will explore the impact we have as radiators of frequency. I will share a story about my cat Crystal and her impact on me. We will discuss your impact on the planet through the following topics:

- Understanding your role as a microcosm of the macrocosm

- How to improve your frequency for yourself and the planet

- Ways to step into your role as a high-frequency resonator

- How to spread high-frequency energy wherever you go

The frequency we hold within, resonates in the world. If we want peace "out there," we must have peace within. The way to make change in the world is to make change within ourselves. If we have anger within, that is what we are going to witness out in the world. If we have sorrow within, that is what we will witness out in the world. And, if we have peace within, that is what we are going to witness in the world.

My Cat as a Relevant Resonator

I believe my cat Crystal is a healer. Her purpose on this planet seems to be to spread healing wherever she goes. She is always with me when I'm working with clients. She helps with clients, and with me personally. If I have a headache, it is very common that I will wake up in the middle of the night with her leaning against my head or splayed across my forehead in some way, purring like a big cat. That frequency of purring, I believe, is intended to assist me in healing. She is very sensitive that way. I've had experiences where I've been very sad, and I wake up in the middle of the night, and she's sleeping on my chest, right above my heart, purring like a finely tuned motor. She is certainly clearing the energy of distress inside my body. Isn't that what we all should be doing?

How can we raise our own frequency and that of the planet?
By developing a deep understanding that we are a microcosm of the macrocosm. One cat can make a difference in the world, and she walks around like she knows it. As we improve our frequency, either independently or with the help of others, we will radiate that higher frequency out into the planet. I invite you to step into your role as a high frequency radiator. What you do, does matter.

Steps and Methods

Raise your frequency for yourself and the planet. Everything is made of energy, from the book you are reading, to the thoughts you are thinking, from the car that you drive, to the emotions that you feel. It is all energy. And everything in our existence is part of an interconnected web of electromagnetic vibrational frequencies. Frequency is measured in hertz (Hz), the rate at which vibrations occur. Frequencies are used to determine and differentiate vibrational patterns. Positive emotions like gratitude, forgiveness, reverence, inspiration, and love have higher frequency, while negative emotions like anxiety, anger, guilt, shame, fear, and despair have lower frequencies.

Trapped emotions stored as pockets of electromagnetic energy in our organs, muscles, and tissues also have a negative frequency and negatively influence our well-being.

Be the high-frequency radiator you are intended to be. Intentionally step into the role of being a high frequency radiator. Everyone who dedicates the time and discipline to change their internal frequency will have a positive effect on the world around them. A vibrant and complete human aura indicates a vital and healthy person. Physical vitality, mental clarity, emotional stability, and highly tuned spiritual energies will result in a larger, brighter, and more protective aura radiance. An unhealthy person's aura is dim and weak. The aura is our first line of defense against detrimental environmental factors. It plays a role in our decision-making and how we communicate nonverbally with other people.

Why be a high frequency radiator?

- The higher the frequency, the more freely your creativity flows

- Being in flow allows us to be more motivated to do what is ours to do

- Higher motivation leads to abundance and the ease of life that comes from that.

- Elevated frequency also allows us to be in a better state of mind, so obstacles don't rock our world as much.

- When everything seems easier, it is also easier to take positive risks.

- And perhaps one of the most important aspects of carrying a higher frequency, is when we feel connected to all that is, our intuitive guidance is clearer.

- It is far easier to follow intuition when our lives are in order.

It's very hard to interpret signals and gut feelings if our lives are difficult, cluttered, or we are living with a lot of discomfort and unrest.

Spread high frequency energy wherever you go. Anytime our frequency is elevated, we feel safer, and more grounded within ourselves, and therefore have more empathy for others. Empathy has the ability to help us recognize our connection to each and every person, plant, and animal on our planet, which is the foundation of oneness.

We can intentionally spread high-frequency energy in the form of love.

- Imagine your heart as the radiant force that it is.

- Visualize each heartbeat flowing an expanding wave of love like a pebble in a pond, out in every direction.

- See smiles on the faces of all the people who experience that love.

- Continue that flow until the entire planet is blanketed with that radiating love.

- See that flow wrapping around the earth in waves that return back to you.

- Feel that love filling you up completely, raising your frequency as you continue flowing outward.

To recap, our lives are made up and influenced by frequency all around us. My hope is that you have gained an understanding of how frequency influences your life and that there are methods you can use to have the experiences you really want in your life.

Chapter 2

Seeking Light from an Abyss of Darkness

Your body stores past physical and emotional traumas as energy. This affects you emotionally and physically. Here we will explore what you can do to move on from the trauma you've experienced. You will see how, through the stories of my own growth, you can grow, too.

I hope you are as eager as I am to cleanse yourself of your past. Remember, you can always find out more about transformational work here.

Your inner ghosts have a stranglehold on your life. We all have emotions from past pain stored within us — often referred to as our inner shadows — that negatively affect our lives in many ways. When these stored emotions are brought forward to be examined and released, our emotional, physical, and spiritual lives dramatically improve.

Here I will discuss the methods I used to uncover, address, and overcome my inner darkness, using these steps:

- What clues can lead you to stored emotions and core shadow beliefs

- What emotions are there, and where are they stored?

- What age were you when you stored that pain?

- Learn the intensity of the trauma and how much trouble it is causing you.

I spent my early years on a farm with my family: my sisters and my parents. My siblings and I were wrapped in the embrace of a vast network of support, protection, and extended family love. We relished this comfort — until our world imploded. I was nine years old when my parents divorced and our entire family (and my heart) was ripped apart.

Mom moved my sisters and me away from this cocoon of love to a place far away from everything we knew. Of course, there were positive experiences after the move, and one of them was being introduced to the Unity Church. The doctrine of this church is all about the power of positive thinking, God is love, and methods of personal development. I was deeply involved in learning the processes of the mind, consciousness, and the way we can control how we think from an early age.

My connection with the Unity Church continued until I was out of college. During all those years, I was surrounded with a deeply positive environment, along with powerful, positive teachings. Beyond that, upon starting my career, I began to take Dale Carnegie classes, which was the premier personal-growth programming of that time.

My experience in the Dale Carnegie program was so powerful that I enrolled in it a couple times and then became an assistant teacher. My life was — and continues to be — an immersion in positive thinking, affirmations, mind manifestos, and positive food for the soul. In my mid-forties, however, I had the sudden realization that I was still struggling with significant levels of self-doubt, low self-esteem, and concerns about who I was and how I appeared to the world. It didn't make sense to me that I would be experiencing this after all the training I'd had.

I had read Susan Shumsky's book, Divine Revelation, in which she describes a process where you can always receive an answer you seek from the Source, every time. I decided to employ her process, and asked myself, "What's with the lack of self-esteem and the impending self-doubt?" Upon asking that question, almost instantly I saw a picture in my mind that I had seen repeatedly over the course of time. Each time it showed up — Oh, there's that memory again!

The picture was a bird's eye perspective of my sisters and me standing next to my father's car on the day of the divorce. Dad was in his car, ready to drive away, saying goodbye to us. I didn't know what the picture meant. This time, I had the wherewithal to say, "I've seen this picture before so many times. What does it mean?" And the words that came into my mind immediately after asking this were, "If your father would leave, it means he doesn't love you. And if he doesn't love you, no one will."

Now I had something to work with. My inner frequency could only rise if my inner perception was of love instead of shame. This became my mission, my purpose. Today, I love my life. I have loving relationships all around me. My life is filled with beautiful friends and beautiful experiences, all because my inner love of self is now overflowing, and my work with others comes from the overflow.

Steps and Methods

The single most important work we can do in our lifetime is to clear out the inner turmoil so Source energy has a clear path to help us reach our highest frequency. The inward process is vital to know what we are dealing with. Here is what you can do:

What clues can lead you to your stored emotions and your core shadow beliefs about yourself? I have used the picture experience with many of my clients. Do you have a picture that keeps popping up, of an experience that happened to you as a child? Even if you don't think it left a painful imprint, it probably did. If you are significantly visual, you may be able to remember something like this. Sometimes there is more than one such experience.

How often do we not pay attention to what triggers us? We often blame it on another person. Unfortunately, blaming another for our emotions is being a victim. When we claim our triggers as our own and take responsibility for our own emotions, we take back our power, and then we can do something about the triggers. Triggers are clues that we have stored emotions.

Whenever we are triggered, an underlying story stored within us causes us to believe something about ourselves that has its origin in our past. Triggers are unexpected physical or emotional "alarms" telling us we have inner pain to deal with and grow through. You will increase your emotional intelligence when you begin to learn from your triggers instead of allowing them to continue to go off unchecked.

What emotions are there, and where are they stored? Good emotions set us on our path to freedom. Low frequency emotions rob us of our joy, and cause us to think there is something wrong with us. We want to locate and work through those to release them. Emotions like grief, sadness, worry, anger, guilt, fear, or shame are culprits that, if left to their own defenses, will cause undue emotional and physical pain.

What age were you when you stored that pain? When you identify the age, and even the incident, it is possible to relate to the little you of that age like the little you is a separate being from the adult you. You need to be the savior of that little one who has been struggling for so long, feeling unseen and unheard. It is a part of you that feels that love goes away. And you are going to be the love that stays for that little you. You are going to be the one who is always there for them, filling their love-cup and guiding them through the perils they have been experiencing.

The intensity of the trauma and the trouble it causes you. I have unearthed many experiences that I had been ignoring. When I touched them in meditation from the perspective of the little one that stored them, the tears flowed hard and heavy for a significant time. Those tears burned off the energy of those buried emotions and released the pain wrapped up in that story. What was the process?

- Sit down in a comfortable location where you will not be disturbed.

- Be certain your spine is straight and your ears are aligned over your shoulders and hips.

- Take three deep, gentle breaths in through your nose, sending your breath to the deepest part of your torso. On each exhalation, relax your body a little bit more. When you feel fully relaxed during the next four exhalations, you will release to the next deeper level of consciousness. Inhale and, exhaling, use your intention and tell yourself, 'I release my conscious mind.' Feel that release as real. Inhale again and, on exhaling, use your intention and say in your mind, 'I release my unconscious mind.' And feel that release. Inhale again, and then exhale, using your intention and saying, 'I release my subconscious mind.' And feel that release. Inhale again, and exhale using your intention and saying in your mind, 'I release any other layers separating me from my highest God self' — and feel that as real.

- On the next inhalation, use your intention to breathe in your highest God self, feeling that happen as real.

- Then ask yourself the question, 'What kind of trauma is affecting me that I need to know about today?'

- And listen. The answer will come in for you in a picture inside your mind, in words from a messenger, or in the form of thoughts.

- If something comes in that you don't understand, ask what it means, and listen again. This is a very effective technique to get the deep truths from your highest Source.

In this aspect, we will discuss and assist you with the foundational reasons for why you do what you do and live the way you live, and think the thoughts that you think.

Is Your Body the Garage of Unclaimed Baggage?

The ghosts of your emotional past have been manipulating your entire world without your knowledge. Your life can improve in infinite ways by uncovering and addressing what was buried so long ago.

Here, we'll explore different ways our past negatively dictates our future, and how we can identify the offending experiences behind this. Then we'll look at what you can use to reveal your own shaming emotional ghosts:

- Are you defending yourself regularly?

- Are you talking to and about yourself in 3rd person?

- Are you a perfectionist?

- Do you judge yourself or others?

You can live with your own ghosts, but why would you? Most of us have some kind of dialogue that runs repeatedly inside our mind, maybe on a loop that repeats over and over again. This dialogue, more often than not, is low-frequency conversation that is very hard on you from a self-esteem standpoint.

I didn't know that this happened until one day I was running and realized I was listening to myself, defending myself for things that I had done. Or what I was planning to do. I was trying to create some kind of a dialogue that would help me feel protected by my decision or something that I had done. In my mind, I was unsure about my actions and decisions. I developed this elaborate story with all these points as to why I did what I did, or would do what I was planning.

That day I realized that this was a pattern of mine. It occurred to me that for years and years I had been listening to myself proving myself over and over. Later, when I was working with one of my spiritual teachers, I discovered that my pattern of defending myself was an indication I had been shamed in monumental ways as a child. I carried a sense of guilt, shame, self-doubt, and discomfort related to every decision I made. I have come to learn with my client work and through my institute students that this is happening in epidemic proportions.

Steps and Methods

Here, I hope to unveil for you the low-frequency energy you're holding in.

While you are not the thoughts that float around in your head, these thoughts can affect you in positive or negative ways. The ongoing negative chatter that plagues so many of us can squash the dreams we strive to create. Understand what you're saying to yourself, and why. Listen closely to identify what kind of conversation your mind is having with you.

A person suffering from toxic shame believes there is something innately wrong with them, that they are "shameful" or "bad." They experience a chronic sense of worthlessness, low self-esteem, and self-loathing. Toxic shame most commonly develops because of childhood experiences. "Shame on you" and "You should be ashamed of yourself" were common phrases heard in my childhood. Shame can also be internalized through similar kinds of experiences at school with our teachers, friends, or other family members. Toxic shame is also caused by extreme forms of abuse like incest, rape, and other forms of sexual assault that cause us to lose our grounding in reality. Sometimes toxic shame develops from later life traumatic experiences such as living in a dysfunctional or abusive relationship, work incidents in which we are humiliated, repeated rejection from other people and organizations, betrayal, and other forms of emotional abuse.

SCAN ME

If you speak to yourself in the third person, you can be disassociating from who you are because it was scary to be you at pivotal times in your life. Other clues to this experience include PTSD, depression or anxiety, gaps of time in your life you don't remember, and detachment from your emotions or emotional numbness, among others. Disassociation or dissociative symptoms usually occur to escape childhood trauma from long-term physical, sexual, or emotional abuse, though it is also prevalent in people who have experienced serious adult trauma, such as experiencing natural disasters, undergoing combat, or enduring being prisoners of war.

If you constantly re-evaluate circumstances, activities and experiences, you tend to be a perfectionist. Perfectionism indicates that you are likely afraid to be fully seen for who you truly are. You are afraid to be authentically you.

Again, this falls back to shame or possibly guilt. You may believe, "If I look perfect, act perfect, work perfect, and live perfect, I can cover up who I really am and can avoid or minimize shame, blame, and judgment." Perfectionism is a shield to protect you from pain. It is a fear that you will somehow not measure up to what you think others think of you. It is a fear to be seen for who you really are, which is a wonderfully flawed human just like the rest of us.

Perfectionism is not the key to success. In fact, research shows perfectionism hampers achievement and is correlated with depression, anxiety, addiction, and life paralysis, or missed opportunities.

The fear of failing, making mistakes, not meeting people's expectations, and being criticized keeps us outside the arena where healthy competition and striving unfolds. Lastly, perfectionism is not a way to avoid shame — it is an illustration of shame.

SCAN ME

When you recognize you are negatively judging others, it's a hallelujah moment. Judging another is a powerful clue that we are also judging ourselves. When you hear yourself being critical of another person or circumstance, you can be certain you are also being equally critical of yourself in ways that are possibly unknown.

If you hear the voices of others speaking to you in your head, either you are seeking validation from others because you believe your own thoughts and opinions are not valuable, or you are disassociating from who you are and those voices are a fractured aspect of you.

The ultimate freedom is to get to a place where the dialogue flowing through you supports who you are and represents your goals. When the dialogue is diminishing, you will continue to struggle in making forward progress in the most productive and prosperous way

Are Your Inner Ghosts Alive?

The emotional traumas of your past negatively influence your life until you realize their impact and become the archeologist of your buried traumatic experiences. Identifying and finding the stored emotions attached to those traumas is the key to unlocking your brightest future.

Here, we will focus on taking the first steps to help you unearth these traumas. With this information, you can then begin the process of healing those traumas, and step into the captain's chair of your future, while letting go of the victimhood of your past.

We will also provide the following tools you can use to begin this healing process:

- Common locations for specific emotions
- How to determine when you stored these emotions
- Important probing questions to uncover the emotional seeds

Upon completing these exercises, you will know your past traumas and how they have been influencing your life, and you will have experienced the deep healing that comes from doing this important work.

First, let's identify your age when and where you first stored these dense emotions.

Steps and Methods

First, where are the emotions stored? The storage of emotions and their effects on a person's life has been researched by the ancient science of medical Qigong for centuries, and by other ancient practices as well. Through Qigong, we learned what the commonly stored emotions are, and where they are commonly stored.

Emotion	Location Stored
Grief	Sinuses & Lungs
Sadness/Heartbreak	Heart
Worry	Stomach & Pancreas
Anger	Liver
Fear	Kidneys & Reproductive organs

I have found this to be a helpful guide in my own practice. I have also found that multiple emotions can be stored in a single area, and that the same emotion can be stored in multiple areas. I adapt this chart for each individual client. The trauma each person experiences is unique to them. To determine the emotion for yourself and others, watch your behavior when your emotions are high. Without harsh judgment, but rather out of a desire to know, ask yourself, "What is the foundational emotion of this behavior?" Sometimes it looks like anger, while the real emotion is fear. Getting to the most primal emotion will allow you to address the emotion directly, and more efficiently.

Next, when were the emotions stored? It's important to determine at which age the emotion was stored so you can effectively release the trauma. Once you have determined the true emotion behind the behavior, then ask yourself, "How old am I behaving?" Once you have received this information, you have the ammunition you need to move forward with the releasing process.

What behaviors are showing up that demonstrate these possibilities? Sometimes you won't find where these emotions are stored. Do not be discouraged. The process can be done successfully without knowing this information. Consider yourself extraordinary! We will master this situation anyway! What other information can help us uncover this information?

Use this chart to indicate your answers. While you are working on this chart, continue to let the information unfold. One answer may not be the only answer. As you write, pay attention to the physical and emotional feelings and memories that show up in your body. These will be clues to the answers you are seeking:

List ways your father positively and/or negatively influenced you?	
List ways your mother positively and/or negatively influenced you.	
List events that left a strong negative impression on your mind.	
What were your personal perceptions about what really happened?	
What core shadow beliefs came out of these perceptions?	
What self-sabotaging behaviors surfaced from these core shadow beliefs?	
List the life circumstances that resulted from your self-sabotaging behavior.	
What is the underlying benefit or self-fulfilling prophesy you are seeking by holding onto your confining beliefs?	

My hope is that you have begun the process of finally healing those emotional traumas and that you continue this work to uncover all the layers of your inner trauma so you can unleash the life you deserve, and impact the world with your most elevated abilities.

Emerging into Freedom

Your past physical and emotional traumas are stored as energy in your body, which creates the foundation from which you live your life. Doing what is necessary to release those traumas once and for all will allow you to experience life from a pure perspective and create your future from a pristine slate. Your health will improve dramatically, and your self-esteem will skyrocket.

Here we are going to explore the most important aspects of releasing the traumas that have hampered your life from the time they occurred. We will do the following exercises to cleanse your inner shadows and open you to your most vibrant existence:

- Call on the wisdom of the little person you were when the trauma occurred.

- Sit with that little person as if they were in the room with you.

- Give them exactly what they needed at the time the trauma occurred.

- Feel into the release that comes from that little one being fully acknowledged in the way they have always needed it.

- Experience your life of freedom from your past traumas.

My hope is that you experience similar tremendous breakthroughs using these techniques to build a life of freedom. This is the work we came to do in this lifetime, so let's start today. Escape the inner turbulence and live a life of freedom.

I had one particular experience during my healing process in which I realized my self-doubt. One day, I was in meditation and using Susan Chomsky's technique, and I quieted my mind and asked what else I needed to release. A little girl's voice came out of my mouth and spoke. She said, "I just want to be loved." I had never known before that it was stored inside. I knew I felt unlovable. My hurt little self kept saying, "I just want to be loved." I was shocked, and feared I might be schizophrenic. But I learned I was not, and I learned to trust this voice I have since called Shelly. Shelly has continued to inform me when I reach out to her. It turns out this is another way you can determine the kind of emotions stored and where they might be located.

These experiences unlocked my inner trauma. My self-concept came from my own self-loathing and negative self-talk. The only person who could love the little me was the big me. When that began to happen in the ways the little me needed, the big me also began to rise out of the darkness of limited self-concept. To expand on her situation, the big me also told me how to heal the emotional traumas in others, as well. So now, my full-time practice is working with people who are being held back from fully living due to traumas that happened when they were young.

Steps and Methods

Here are some healing techniques:

Go to your emotional inner child. The journey out of suffering and back home to yourself involves learning to love all aspects of yourself. The greatest suffering comes from your lack of ability or willingness to have love and compassion for yourself whenever you are in physical, emotional, or spiritual pain. Denying yourself the expression of that love and compassion immeasurably amplifies the pain you are already suffering. Anger, hatred, frustration, shame, and ultimately depression are all results of this denial. Wounds, traumas, and wrong conclusions from past experiences are triggers and doorways used by unseen negative influences to create division.

Determine what nurturing this inner child has needed for so long and has never received. Become the Divine Mother and Father to your hurt inner child. You are the wisdom carrier of the exact words and self-loving actions your inner child needs to receive from yourself for healing of your deepest wounds.

Provide your inner child the words, the expressions of love and the support that are unique to them. Fill their proverbial love cup so they are no longer stuck in a cycle of repeated pain and suffering, and as you make a daily practice of honoring all parts of yourself you eventually become whole in your relationship with yourself. This depth of compassion for yourself is the foundation for you to embody your highest frequency and eventually generates an overflowing compassion for all beings in your path. A deep love of yourself is the path to inner peace, and the path to uplift and heal the world. You should initiate these important steps. When you do, you will experience the empowering breakthroughs I have, and your dream of a life of freedom will be your reality. Let's start today to master this important task and rise up to the truth of who you really are.

Steps Toward Freedom	Action for You
1. Call on the wisdom of your inner child through meditation.	Ask your inner child to reveal to you what trauma or traumas are present, where healing needs to occur.
2. Experience/pretend this child is right there with you as a separate individual in the room.	Feel into their presence. Determine what they need to feel whole? Is it to be held? To be honored? To be heard? To be unconditionally loved? To be spoken to with tender respect?

3. Provide your inner child exactly what they need and have needed for so long.	• Earn your inner child's trust slowly. Often they do not trust adults since adults caused their original pain. • Flow a continuous wave of love from your heart to their heart. • Communicate to them telepathically that you're here for them and will honor them in every possible way. • Speak words of love and compassion that they need to hear. • Ask what they would like to know or experience, and then provide that for them. • Pay attention to them and play with them as you would with an invisible friend. • Continue until you experience a sense of completion, or they have risen into a state of pure innocence related to that original wound. This can take weeks or more. • Repeat. We hold many layers and experiences of stuck emotions. With the release of each trauma, we experience more and more inner freedom. • Allow emotions and tears to emerge and flow. Express anger safely. Allow yourself to feel fear fully.
4. Feel into the release that comes from that little one being fully acknowledged in the way they have always needed.	• When you come out on the other side of these emotions, the breakthrough has happened. Burning the fuel of the emotions is vital to the process. The energy is burned out and a new life can emerge.

| 5. Experience your life of freedom. | • The feeling of unfettered freedom springs forth when the discharge from your emotions is no longer felt. |
| | • You feel like a new person because you are experiencing life from an entirely different perspective. |

Chapter 3

Is Your Home a Hazardous Waste Receptacle?

We all want a happy and safe home. But far too often we unintentionally create an unsafe and potentially toxic environment in our home, yard, and family environment.

Unnatural products cannot vibrate at a health-supporting frequency. They can introduce poison and emit a damaging frequency into the environment. In this chapter, we explore clearing your home of synthetic chemicals so that you can dramatically improve your future health, and that of your children and pets.

Here, we will explore the myriad of ways you could be polluting your home and the necessary adjustments you can make to improve your home environment. We will discuss the most significant areas of your home to address. These include:

- Removing synthetic or unnatural chemicals.

- Replacing them with natural options.

- Removing your shoes at the door.

- Proper care of your carpets and household surfaces.

- Addressing the incoherent electromagnetic frequencies.

Because the frequency in my home is elevated, animals like to get as close as they can to my home. One summer years ago, I was hearing someone walking on my ceiling. My home has a cathedral ceiling, so there is only a small gap between the ceiling and the roof. I kept hearing walking on my ceiling. After a few weeks of listening to these footsteps, I began hearing the sound of babies grunting and nursing. It seemed as if I now had a family living in the wall! Still, it didn't seem to be a big problem. Until the odor of wild animals — and the strong smell of urine — began to permeate the walls. It was clear I had to initiate an extraction process.

I called the humane wildlife service to catch these creatures, which turned out to be racoons, and take them somewhere else to make a home. These crafty racoons moved around within the walls. It took around five weeks for these creatures to be extracted.

The reason I tell you this story is that now I have this horrible odor in my home because of the mess that the raccoons left in the wall. Our solution was to use Young Living Thieves Household Cleaner, a mixture of natural products, including clove, cinnamon, lemon, eucalyptus, and rosemary essential oils. These natural substances also provide excellent disinfection due to their natural antiseptic, antimicrobial, bactericidal, antiviral, and anti-infectious properties.

The mission was to clear any harmful bacteria and kill those odors. This product did the trick, and I have given this blessing to myself, my pets, and my home for many years. Anyone coming in to do any kind of work is not allowed to use chemicals of any kind.

Steps and Methods

Here are some ways to deal with such toxic chemicals:

Eliminate all non-natural chemical products in your home. Many laundry and dishwashing detergents, as well as most products with fragrances, contain endocrine disruptors, chemicals that interfere with the body's hormone functions. While there is a low risk that any given exposure will result in immediate negative health outcomes, constant repeated exposure increases the risk of harm.

Replace harmful products with natural options. Most of us have become accustomed to running to the store for whatever supplies we need. While there are natural or green solutions available for cleaning your home at the market, you do not have to walk down a cleaning aisle to find your best options for cleaning your home. Open your pantry for excellent natural cleaning options.

Create a space at your entrance to leave street shoes and house slippers. Wear your slippers in the house. According to a recent University of Houston study, more than 26% of shoes worn inside the home are contaminated with Clostridium difficile (C. diff), a bacterium that can cause stomach pain and explosive diarrhea. In many Asian countries, shoes are never worn inside.

It is wise to just slip off your shoes at the door and regularly deep clean your entryway with natural cleanser to be certain that chemicals are kept outside.

Clean your carpets and surfaces with the natural products initially to remove the chemicals. Where do we start? If you are just entering into the green cleanser arena, start by getting rid of your commercially prepared, VOC-laden cleaning products. Use your natural products and systematically clean all your carpets and surfaces.

Reduce the electromagnetic frequency (EMF) incoherence in your home. All electrical devices in your home such as lamps, televisions, computers, phones, microwaves, wi-fi routers, etc., emit electromagnetic vibrational frequencies that are incoherent and chaotic to our bodies.

There are multiple ways to reduce the harmful influence and protect yourself from EMF stress. The simplest one is to minimize the usage of your electronic devices. However, in our age of sophisticated technologies, that seems to be impossible. Most people can't imagine their life without their smartphones and computers. So we can, instead, make their usage safer and less harmful for health.

The most efficient and cheapest way to reduce radiation influence is through the use of shungite. Shungite is a crystal stone widely known for its absorbing and protecting properties. Shungite is a natural magnetic material with a strong screening effect that neutralizes high frequency and microwave frequency electromagnetic radiation.

I have shungite crystals next to each one of my wireless devices and in my bedroom for protection when I'm sleeping. As I shared before, my phone had very low EMF emissions when I tested it. The reason for that is because I have a shungite disc on it. We tested my friend's cell phone without any shungite protection and the emissions were drastically higher. Since doing the testing, I have doubled up on the shungite around my wifi and put it on a timer so it turns off automatically at night. Our bodies are more susceptible to the damage of EMF emissions when we sleep.

Take inventory of steps you know you are ready to take, and

record them, perhaps in your diary. To connect with more opportunities to raise your frequency and enhance your life, go here.

Is Your Yard a Toxic Dump?

One of the most important ways to ensure a safe living environment is to be intentional about the chemicals that are put on your lawn. Yard care products have some of the most hazardous types of carcinogens and are overlooked from a health standpoint. We will address three important considerations for a healthy lawn:

- Cease and desist using weed killers of any kind.

- Use natural and organic fertilizer.

- Use organic soil when potting plants, gardening or adding fill soil.

When you employ these basic concepts into your lawn and garden care, you will be improving your home environment, the future health of your loved ones, and gaining a more compassionate relationship with mother earth.

I received a message of caution while meditating, during a period when I was having my pool torn out and the hole filled in. I had a 19 ft X 39 ft, 8.5 ft deep in-ground swimming pool. Due to drainage complications and other significant inconveniences, I decided to take out all the structural aspects of the pool, fill in the huge hole, and turn the yard into a meditation oasis. One day during meditation, I received a message that I needed to be concerned about what the excavation crew was using to fill the hole. I called my landscaper to find out what he was planning to use. I was pleased with his general concern, especially after I told him about my meditation. During the meditation, the feeling of illness came over me when I thought about what kind of fill they were putting into the pool space. My yard has been a sanctuary for people, animals, birds, toads, and all manner of random creatures. I have not used chemicals there for decades. The service people didn't know what they were putting in the hole, in terms of chemicals. They had been told it was safe for animals and children. But we need to be more mindful than that.

Most commonly used lawn pesticides are dangerous to human health. It truly matters how we choose to treat our lawns, landscape, and plants.

Steps and Methods

Stop putting weed killer of any kind on your lawn. Weed killers are filled with carcinogens. According to Stefan Sobkowiak, weeds grow in our yards when the soil is depleted of minerals that the weed will provide to the soil. Feeding your soil with organic compost or other natural fertilizers is a much healthier idea than killing the weeds.

Fertilize your yard and plants with natural organic products. There are several commercially available natural organic fertilizers you can use. For many years I have been using an organic product called Sustane 4-6-4 to fertilize my lawn, flowers, and bushes with excellent results.

Use organic soil when potting plants, gardening or adding fill soil. Commercially prepared potting soils, top soil, and other fill dirt can come from sources that have been treated with chemicals for weed control and other reasons. There are organic soils available to use for most purposes, and they will provide a safe environment for all who may wander through the areas they are used in. When gardening, this is your only good choice.

Candles, Renuzit, and Swiffers — Oh, My!

Our world is inundated with feel-good marketing for products that do not support good health. We buy into the experience they paint for us because, as compassionate people, we believe what they are telling us. The basic rule to abide by is that nothing synthetic supports health frequencies.

Here we will explore establishing rules of safety for your home and personal care products. I give you these tips for improving your home environment:

- Always read the labels of environment "enhancing" products before making a purchase.

- Use soy and beeswax candles with pure essential oil fragrance.

- Just say "no" to air fresheners and odor eliminators.

Years ago, before I really understood the significance of chemicals in home products, one of my girlfriends would come over regularly because I hosted events in my home, which also doubles as the Infinite Living Center of Holistic Experience. Sometimes when Julie came over, she would become very agitated. Her eyes would begin to itch. Her sinuses would act up. She'd get a headache and have difficulty breathing.

One day, as she walked around the center, she said, "There it is." She pointed at some candles that were burning and told me these were products that were irritating her system. Since then, we use beeswax or soy candles, not petroleum-based ones. They are so much better for the environment. The problem was the fragrance. In most candles, the fragrance is synthetic. Synthetic fragrances are made of chemicals that can be problematic from a health standpoint.

Steps and Methods

Here are a few tips:

Always read labels. If there are words you cannot pronounce, there are unwanted chemicals in them. Many of these products have volatile organic compounds (VOCs) that have been proven to be carcinogenic. Fragrances made from chemicals may cause health challenges.

Use soy or beeswax candles with high grade essential oil fragrance and natural wicks. The benefits of using candles made of natural products outweigh the increased costs, and provide better air quality, with fewer health hazards. Natural wax candles burn longer, and may not actually be more expensive to burn. Organic waxes, such as soy wax or beeswax, help prevent exposure to harsh, potentially harmful chemicals.

Beware of air fresheners and odor eliminators. One easy way to improve the air quality in your home is by switching from conventional air fresheners and odor eliminators to healthier options. In studies measuring the different substances that air fresheners emit, researchers have found numerous chemicals associated with toxic effects. I looked into Febreze as well, and while the company would only disclose three ingredients, the Environmental Working Group (EWG) found 87 chemicals in the Febreze Air Effects product, many of which are neurotoxins, endocrine disruptors, and known to cause cancer and many other health challenges.

Don't trust the "green" ones, either. One research organization tested products labeled "all natural" and found that 86% of the products tested contained one or more phthalates. Many phthalates are toxic substances linked to breast cancer and endocrine disruption. Such products hardly constitute "all natural," "green," or "clean." Most people prefer a fragrance-free environment, but if you want to add fragrance to your home, healthy alternatives include diffusing high quality essential oils (not the ones on the grocery shelf or at the gas station) or simmering herbs like cinnamon and cloves.

Use this information for the purpose it was intended, to truly enhance your life by safely disposing of all the synthetic chemicals in your home, and replacing them with true life-enhancing natural products.

Energy Flow Is Serious Business

The flow of energy in and around your house can significantly impact your overall health, wealth, and happiness. Many Asian cultures have known this for centuries and apply what the Chinese refer to as Feng Shui in their daily lives.

Here we will discuss the impact that energy flow can have, and how you can use it in your home and your life to your highest advantage. We will provide these basic guidelines you can use to improve the flow of energy in your home:

- Less is always more.

- Does this feel like a VIP lives here?

- Long hallways drain energy.

- No more poison arrows.

- Only calming energy for your bedroom.

I have been studying Qigong for many, many years and my Qigong Master, Chunyi Lin, who is also a Fung Shui master, shared with me a story of a family that wanted its home evaluated from a Feng Shui standpoint.

The first thing Chunyi noticed when he walked up to his client's house was a tree in the yard directly aligned with the front door,, which was blocking the view. Chunyi moved about the home, evaluating the layout of the house and the placement of furniture in each room. Based on his assessment, he told the family that most people in the household had either sinus problems or an ongoing cough. He said that certain of them had lower-back pain, and described the family's various ailments resulting from the energy-flow pattern in their home. The tree that was directly in front of their front door blocked the energy flow in the throat of the house — there wasn't a clear flow of energy in and out of the "mouth" of the house. The backache was a result of clutter, and was probably also a result of the way furniture was placed in a certain room.

The placement of our furniture, the way that a door is exposed to the street, whether or not we have stairs inside our front door, what we see when we enter our home — all have an effect, not only on the energy flow but also on the health of those who live there. Some of this can be corrected, using crystals to redirect the energy, and there are other methods available.

The Chinese concept of feng shui is becoming better known in the western world. While I am not a feng shui expert, I can still offer you some basic concepts to set the stage for better energy flow in your home.

Steps and Methods

Less is more. Clutter blocks the flow of energy. Eliminate it. Clutter indicates a decision that was not made in a timely way, so a stack was created. Get in the habit of making a decision to toss it in the trash or put it in its intended storage location.

Establish a philosophy that your home is supporting the VIP who lives there. Stand in the corners and look out into the rooms to see if what you see represents what you want in your life. If not, make changes .

Change the flow of rushing energy down long hallways or downstairs by dangling crystal prisms from the ceiling in that area. It will disrupt the flow and produce harmony.

Corners where two walls come together to create an outward pointing arrow produce energy flow in sharp points. This is irritating to our energy fields and can produce physical and emotional circumstances. Soften those edges with rounded corner guards and the flow of energy will reduce disturbance in your home.

As your sleep sanctuary, your bedroom should not have heavy energy in it, such as big stereos or televisions. And if you are a couple or wanting to be a couple, you should have one bed and two of everything else, i.e., night stands, lamps, places to store clothes, etc. This will either bring in a relationship, or enhance the one you are in.

Raising the Frequency of Your Home

Most of us are sensible about spaces. We know if something feels off. The exception may be our own homes — since we are there so much, we get numb to its frequency. Our homes carry the frequency of what has happened or is happening inside those walls. That frequency is a catalyst bringing more of the same frequency to you.

Here we will explore ways you can improve your home's frequency so it will support the life you desire. I will share the story of the frequency shift of my own home, and provide you the following ways to start today to make your home's frequency match the life of your dreams:

- Meditate.

- Loop a mantra 24/7.

- Add crystals in every room.

- Diffuse pure essential oils.

- Keep your emotions in check.

- Say "no" to the mainstream news.

When I first walked into my house as a potential buyer, I knew immediately it was my home. That was 27 years ago. When I first moved in, my furnishings were quite dark, in fact, actually black. The accent colors were bright red, more black, and silver. I was very comfortable surrounded by those colors.

My home has always been my spiritual sanctuary, but it has evolved over the years. Recently, I changed to all-white furniture. My walls went from all light gray, to gold. So now the color scheme in my home is white and gold. I realize now this is a demonstration of the consciousness that I have gone through, which is projected through my home.

The frequency of my home at the time I first moved in 27 years ago, and for many years after that, was related to the lowest chakras or energy centers of the body. My Spirit was trying to get me back into my body. Due to stored trauma in my body, my Spirit did not want to stay in there, and it would hover above my head most of the time. The colors were resonant with the lowest chakras to get me grounded. They were black for earth, and red for the root chakra, the one at the bottom of the body. These colors encouraged my Spirit to settle down into my body.

Over the course of time, after engaging in significant personal inner work, my Spirit is now fully grounded in my body. This allows my Spirit to elevate into the highest chakras, which include the crown chakra at the top of the head, and above. The crown chakra is represented by white and the chakra above that is the God chakra, which is represented by gold.

What are the colors in your home? What is the energy in your home? It is to your best benefit to elevate that energy as much as possible. This can be done in a variety of ways, which are illustrated here.

Steps and Methods

This is my favorite mission. My home's energy is very high because I have intentionally added things to enhance it in a maximum way. What can you do to enhance your home's energy?

Meditate or otherwise connect with our infinite Source daily. Do this in the same place every time. Over the course of a short period of time, you will begin to notice the energy in that space feels very pleasing.

Play an Om chant continuously for a year or more at a low volume in your home. Om is the highest frequency vibration and will penetrate the bones of your home over the course of time. My favorite Om chant is Johnathon Goldmans' Ultimate Ohm, available on Spotify or by CD.

Add earth elements, such as crystals, in every room. My house has crystals elegantly placed in every room. Crystals provide many positive frequencies to your home, and amplify the energy. If your energy is good, amplifying it is a great idea.

Use diffusers with the highest-grade essential oils throughout your home. This purifies the air and adds high frequency fragrance that initiates good emotions in people. My favorites are Young Living Essential Oils. They have proven their superior quality over the several years I have affiliated with them.

Be mindful not to "throw negative emotions around." Our emotions can enhance or diminish the frequency of our home. People who are peaceful will produce a peaceful energy in their home. Of course, the opposite is true as well.

Do not watch the news on television or your computer. This is detrimental energy that can ruin your efforts to elevate your home's frequency quite quickly. I have not had a television in my home for over 15 years, just for that reason.

What changes are you inspired to get started on? Find more fun at

Infinite Living.

Chapter 4

What on Earth Are You Eating?

We are what we eat. And we eat a lot that isn't good for us.

I will share my own personal research related to food options, such as the following tools to use to upgrade your food choices:

- How to measure the level of consciousness of food

- High frequency nutritional supplement choices for you

- How to measure the vibrational frequency of food.

- Foods to avoid completely

I have done a great deal of research on the frequencies associated with food.

You would have to be completely out of touch in life not to have some idea what food is better for you, and what foods should be consumed on a limited basis.

Steps and Methods

With that in mind, let's discuss how to measure the frequency of food on the scale of consciousness developed by Dr. David Hawkins:

Level	Scale (Log of)	Emotion	Process	Life-View
Enlightenment	700-1,000	Ineffable	Pure Consciousness	Is
Peace	600	Bliss	Illumination	Perfect
Joy	540	Serenity	Transfiguration	Complete
Love	500	Reverence	Revelation	Benign
Reason	400	Understanding	Abstraction	Meaningful
Acceptance	350	Forgiveness	Transcendence	Harmonious
Willingness	310	Optimism	Intention	Hopeful
Neutrality	250	Trust	Release	Satisfactory
Courage	200	Affirmation	Empowerment	Feasible
Pride	175	Dignity (Scorn)	Inflation	Demanding
Anger	150	Hate	Aggression	Antagonistic
Desire	125	Craving	Enslavement	Disappointing
Fear	100	Anxiety	Withdrawal	Frightening
Grief	75	Regret	Despondency	Tragic
Apathy	50	Despire	Abdication	Hopeless
Guilt	30	Blame	Destruction	Condemnation (Evil)
Shame	20	Humiliation	Elimination	Miserable

POWER: Enlightenment through Courage
FORCE: Pride through Shame

OMEGA — Ultimate Consciousness

Enlightenment 700
Peace 600
Joy 540
Love 500 — Expanded
Reason 400
Acceptance 350
Willingness 310
Neutrality 250
Courage 200
Pride 175
Anger 150
Desire 125
Fear 100 — Contracted
Grief 75
Apathy 50
Guilt 30
Shame 20

ALPHA POINT

Scale of Consciousness Chart

I often use the body resonance techniques Hawkins used that he called kinesiology. I call it muscle testing.

Food can be categorized by levels of consciousness. To determine the level of consciousness a food falls under, select the food you want to test. There are several muscle testing options you can use to determine what your "strong" or "Yes" is. I like to use the whole body technique, in which you stand straight, with your feet being shoulders width apart.

A sense of being pulled forward indicates a 'Yes" answer and a sense of being pulled backward is a "No" answer. Next, you hold the item next to your heart, or just think of an item you want to test. Ask the Universe, "On the 1,000-point scale, where 200 equals Truth and 500 equals love, does the frequency of this food resonate at 200 or above?" Then let your body respond.

Chart of Vibrational Frequencies for Different Foods

Food	Store bought Reg	Store bought Org	Farmer's Market Org
Apples	165	315	515
Strawberries	160	315	560
Carrots-whole	310	310	380
Blueberries	180	490	680
Spinach	290	370	660
Kale	370	540	695
Broccoli	195	370	660
Sweet Potatoes	230	445	560
Juice Plus Trio 850	Fruit/Veggie Blends 850	Berry Blend 860	

If your body is pulled forward, you have an affirmative answer. Repeat the question at intervals of 100 until you get a weak response. Now you know the frequency of that food is between the number where you tested strong, and the number where you tested weak. Continue this process until an ideal number is determined. I tested a number of food items from the store, regular, from the store, organic, and from our farmer's market. The chart offers a list of some of the items I tested.

Another classification of food is vibrational frequency, a measurement of the electrical energy that is present in all natural living things. Royal Raymond Rife, M.D., developed a "frequency generator" in the early 1920s.

Rife found that certain frequencies could destroy a cancer cell or a virus — some could prevent the development of disease, and others would destroy disease. Bruce Tainio of Tainio Technology in Cheney, Washington, developed equipment to measure the biofrequency of humans and foods. He used this biofrequency monitor to determine the relationship between frequency and disease. He measured people, food, thoughts, and other aspects of life that might affect health. It was determined that food can help or hinder our health, depending on its vibrational frequency.

Food can also assist the body in moving energy effectively and efficiently, provided we eat the right types of foods. All foods in their natural state have this vibrational frequency. It is measured in megahertz (MHz) and is a measurement of energy related to bio-electricity and indirectly related to prana (oriental breathing exercise), or vital energy. One hertz is one cycle per second of energy flow that is constant between two points. A healthy human body has a vibrational frequency of 62-68 MHz. Illness begins to set in when our frequency drops to 58 MHz. More serious illness 48-55 MHz and cancer sets in at 42 MHz. If we are a collective frequency of all aspects of our life, including the food we eat, it is vital to feed our bodies foods with the highest vibrational frequency.

To illustrate the sensitivity of our vibrational frequency, let me provide this illustration: In one study, the frequency of two individuals — the first a 26year-old male and the second a 24-year- old male — was measured at 66 MHz each. The first individual held a cup of coffee (without drinking any), and his frequency dropped to 58 MHz in 3 seconds. He put the coffee down and inhaled an aroma of essential oils. Within 21 seconds, his frequency had returned to 66 MHz.

The second individual took a sip of coffee, and his frequency dropped to 52 MHz in the same 3 seconds. However, no essential oils were used during the recovery time, and it took 3 days for his frequency to return to its initial 66 MHz.

The table below illustrates the vibration levels of canned and processed foods and certain unprocessed foods.

Vibrational Level of Food Groups

Vibrational Level of Food Groups	
Food Group	Vibrational Frequency in Megahertz
Canned foods	0-15 MHz
Processed foods	0 MHz
Genetically Modified Foods (GMO)	0 MHz
Fresh Produce	15-22 MHz
Fresh Herbs	20-27 MHz
Dried Herbs	2-22 MHz

Chart of Vibration Levels of Canned, Processed, and Unprocessed Foods

Chart of Vibration Levels of Canned, Processed, and Unprocessed Foods

If we want to live a healthy life filled with vitality, we must eat food that is alive. Just looking at the above chart, you can determine which foods are alive and which are not.

Avoid foods with little to no vibrational value. These include any processed foods, white flour, processed sugar, canned foods, pop, frozen foods, and especially fast foods because they contain most if not all of the above items. Other items to avoid with either no or little vibrational value include cigarettes; hard liquor; pasteurized cow's milk; infant formulas; pharmaceutical drugs; radiation of any kind (X-rays, for example); pasteurized yogurt and cheese; most meats, such as beef, chicken, lamb, and pork; microwaved food; genetically modified food; any artificial sweeteners; margarine and lards; and any foods containing additives.

Foods high in vibration are fresh organic fruits and vegetables, pure clean water, sea vegetation, and raw honey. Other foods that have good vibrational value include maple syrup, cooked vegetables (blanch them to retain optimum vibration), raw nuts and seeds, raw organic dairy products (not pasteurized), free-range eggs, wild fish, and raw oils, such as cold, pressed, extra virgin olive oil, among others.

When eating fresh fruits and vegetables off the plant, tree, or vine, the vibrational benefit of the food is maximized. The sun is the key to everything, as it charges these foods to reach their maximum health benefit. Foods shipped long distances lose their vibrational value by being picked long before they ripen (and therefore have less sun time), and by losing frequency as they travel before they arrive in your kitchen.

Give thanks and bless your food before eating it, and even while preparing and cooking it. It's a good idea to make your kitchen a special, almost sacred place. This will lift the vibration of the food.

It's also important to create an ambiance of peace in the kitchen, especially while preparing food and eating. Other positive meal ideas: Do not argue at the dinner table, eat food slowly, and chew well. This will avail the highest frequency in your food, and enable proper digestion.

I invite you to evaluate your body's resonance, and give it the upgrade it deserves by starting to take action today. Your body and spirit will thank you.

The Truth about Your Bathroom Habits

According to the traditional Hindu system of Ayurveda, compromised digestion is the root cause of ALL illness. If that is true, it is vital to take care of our digestion.

Here we will explore ancient secrets to cleanse and heal your digestive system. I will provide you with several Ayurvedic suggestions for enhancing your digestion:

- Your eating environment is vital.

- Turn up your digestive fire before your meals.

- Cold drinks take digestion to a screeching halt.

- Add detoxifying foods to your regular meals.

- Eat your final meal based on the season.

During more than a year of pandemic-related isolation and distancing, people were less active and put on what they may have jokingly referred to as Covid-weight. I put on a few pounds, too. My activity level was lower than it had ever been. And while I was making reasonable food selections, because of the lack of activity, I was gaining weight for the first time ever.

As serendipity would have it, during this time I was also introduced to a book, Ancient Secrets of A Master Healer, by Dr. Clint G Rogers. This book details a detox program that includes mostly eating mung bean soup. But simply adding mung bean soup to your diet can dramatically change your health for the better in just a few short days. Because mung beans have the highest toxin absorption rate of any food, they can quickly improve a person's health. By eating mung bean soup, I lost the 10 pounds that I had gained during isolation and an additional two pounds that must have been unneeded weight.

Though weight loss was not the reason I was doing the detox, it was a powerful motivator. My real reason for doing it was because I was having abdominal pain on a regular basis. I felt quite certain it was digestive pain because it flared up when I ate certain foods, like chocolate. Following the guidance in this book and consulting with the doctors at the Ayushakti Clinic in India, and doing this detox, I was able to regain my health. The pain in my lower abdomen is no longer there. I can imagine if my digestive pain went away, many other positive things occurred in my body as well. You can improve the flow through your whole system and your life.

Digestive issues are the leading cause of all illness. They masquerade as many different challenges and our western medicine system is not trained to consider overall digestion as the cause of various ailments.

Steps and Methods

Ayurvedic doctors believe that digestion is the root of ALL diseases, and symptoms show up early as indicators we need to make changes. Gastrointestinal discomfort. Excessive odorous gas.

Food allergies and sensitivity. Depression and anxiety. Joint pain and stiffness. Weight gain. Immune system related ailments. If these are symptoms you have, it is time to look into ways to improve your digestion.

Some basic Ayurvedic suggestions to improve and heal your digestion:

- Eat sitting down, in a settled environment, without other distractions, except gentle conversation. Our digestion improves when we are calm and focused on the meal we are eating. Stress alters the chemistry of our digestive juices and reduces the ability for our digestive system to do its work.

- Eat a fresh piece of ginger and lemon before a full meal to ignite the agni and prepare your body for digestion. These foods are heat-producing foods and are helpful to the entire digestive process. If you have digestive issues, avoid the lemon, but definitely include the ginger.

- Avoid ice-cold drinks and food. It puts out your digestive agni, the digestive fire responsible for igniting your digestion. It is helpful to drink a hot cup of water first thing in the morning and last thing before retiring for the night to assist digestion during both parts of the day.

- Add detoxifying foods to your regular meals. Mung beans are a staple in my diet now. Nearly every day I include mung beans in a recipe of soup, a casserole, or as a stand alone dish with health supporting spices such as cumin, coriander, turmeric, and ginger. Other detoxifying foods are fresh veggies that are lightly cooked. Many people advocate raw veggies as the only way. While eating raw is very good for very healthy people, raw veggies are also very difficult to digest. If your digestion is compromised in any way, your digestive system will struggle to digest it properly.

- Eating your final meal of the day before dark and retiring by 10 pm is the best practice, according to the biorhythms of our bodies. Since that is not always easy to do, at least finish eating three or more hours before retiring for the night. Eating too late sets you up for indigestion due to food sitting in your stomach when you are lying down and prevents natural body detoxification.

The ancient medical science of Ayurveda has proven itself over the course of a few thousand years. As the most effective program I have used, I invite you to try the ancient medical secrets program of Ayurveda before any other.

Your Eating Habits Have Grave Consequences

Here, we'll explore dietary mistakes we can easily make. I will share the story of my first iridology appointment (medical diagnosis through examining the iris of the eye) and what changes I made after it. And we will discuss what foods to absolutely say "no" to, such as:

- Trans fats

- Food dyes

- High fructose corn syrup in its many names

- Pesticide-laden fruits and veggies

My hope is that the more you know about what you eat, the more easily you can live a long, healthy, high-frequency life.

Poor digestion can come about in a variety of different ways, often because we consume foods that our bodies can't digest. It is vital that we clean up our diets. Cardiovascular issues take away the quality of our lives, and are the leading cause of death in the world. Start with a good list of ingredients for your diet, and then make good choices to give your body the best opportunity for healthy digestion.

Steps and Methods

We are exposed to so many toxins in day-to-day life, so it is best for us to reduce the insult to our bodies which are easily avoided by making wise choices with our food intake. "Every food can be a medicine or a poison, depending on how you use it," said Dr. Pankaj Naram, an Ayurveda master who passed away in 2020. Some of the most significant things to watch for, and absolutely say no to, include:

Avoid trans fats. They have many names, such as partially or fully hydrogenated oils and more recently under the names mono- and diglycerides. According to Healthline.com, trans fats have no known food value, and can elevate "bad" cholesterol, cause heart disease, and increase inflammation in the body. .

Products categories to watch out for that contain trans fat, include:

- Store and bakery-bought baked goods, such as cakes, cookies, pies, and commercially prepared home baked goods, such as refrigerated dough, biscuits, and rolls, as well as canned frosting.

- Vegetable shortening, margarine, palm oil, canola, corn, soybean oils

- Microwave popcorn

- Fried and grilled fast foods, including hamburgers, french fries, tortillas, doughnuts, and fried chicken, among others

- Non-dairy coffee creamers, also known as coffee whiteners; the main ingredients in most non-dairy coffee creamers are sugar and hydrogenated oil.

- Snacks and pizza. Some brands of potato and corn chips still contain trans fats, as do some brands of crackers and other snacks. Trans fats can be found in some brands of pizza dough. Keep a lookout for partially hydrogenated oil, especially in frozen pizzas.

Avoid food dyes. Food dyes of any kind are linked to cancer and neurocognitive behavioral issues, along with a host of other health threats. In the early 1900s, it became common for U.S. food manufacturers to add artificial coloring or dyes to foods. The use of artificial food coloring has been steadily increasing since the 1950s. Within the past 50 years, the amount of synthetic dye used in foods has increased by 500%!

Avoid high-fructose corn syrup. High fructose corn syrup (HFCS) has been used in more and more processed foods over the last few decades. It's cheaper and sweeter than regular sugar, and is more quickly absorbed into your body. These benefits naturally come with significant risks as well. So far we know, eating too much high fructose corn syrup can lead to insulin resistance, obesity, type 2 diabetes, and high blood pressure.

It is difficult to gauge how much of HFCS we are consuming because it is now hidden under many different names. Here are some of them:

- Maize syrup

- Glucose syrup

- Glucose/fructose syrup

- Tapioca syrup

- Dahlia syrup

- Fruit fructose

- Fructose

Grocery store produce may contain dangerous chemicals.
The list of pesticides that have been found on the produce we eat is long and scary. The effects of long term consumption of those pesticides can be deadly. My personal recommendation is to choose organic, whenever possible.

Restart Your Whole Body by Detoxing

Detoxing our bodies is vitally important to maintaining our overall health and quality of life. When I became familiar with the concept and exercised my first detox program, my health outlook did a complete turnaround.

Here, we will explore detoxing your body. I will share effective detoxification programs that I have used and am very comfortable recommending to you:

- High quality fresh fruits and veggies

- Dr. Moritz's Ultimate Liver Cleanse

- Dr Christopher's Shade Push/Catch Detox System

- The Ancient Secrets of the Mung Bean Soup Detox Program

I began to understand the idea and purpose of detoxification about 10 years ago. My first detox was the most aggressive. It was Dr. Moritz's liver cleanse, from his book of the same name. I have been a clean, healthy, conscious eater for my whole life. The program entails a variety of things like drinking apple juice for six days, followed by a regimen of epsom salts and a concoction of olive oil and grapefruit juice.

The elimination of toxic byproducts is a two-day affair beginning with all the solids in your intestines and then the gallstones that have been building up over the course of my entire life, I suppose.

I did this experience as guided by the book every three weeks for a total of seven times. Once you begin the process, it is recommended to do it every three weeks until there are no more stones in the last experience. I was shocked at what was coming out of my body with regard to gallstones. Over the course of all seven processes, more than two cups of stones were eliminated, and there may have been more than that, since I didn't measure them exactly. I did capture them so I could get a good idea of what was coming out. The stone sizes were astonishing, as well. There were stones that were one and a quarter inches big, and maybe five to ten of those and other stones that varied in size from ¾ inch, to small pea-sized, and many even smaller than that.

I was shocked at the quantity, because I have always eaten so well. I may be able to attribute all of this to the trans fats I had eaten for so many years without realizing their negative effects. I felt amazing after that 7-series experience. Of the four detox systems I have used, that one was the most significant test of my will and well worth it, judging from the final result. It demonstrated to me in a very colorful way what had been going on inside me, and the struggles that my liver and my gallbladder were having, even though I didn't have any symptoms of it.

Steps and Methods

I have used four different systems for myself and my clients that I feel comfortable recommending. Each varies in intensity, and I use each at different times. Though I am a sports medicine professional, and have been for 35 years, I am not a medical doctor. So please consult with your doctor before embarking on any detoxification programs.

The mildest detox is eating high quality fresh vegetables, fruits, and berries daily. Unfortunately, I have found it to be difficult to get the high quality from the produce in our grocery store throughout the year due to living in a 4-season part of the world. The produce has to be transported thousands of miles to get to us more than six months out of the year. And it is nearly impossible to eat the quantity of produce to get the micro nutrients our bodies need.

For these reasons, I found the use of Juice Plus Fruit, Vegetable and Berry blend capsules in my daily routine has guaranteed that I get the highest quality veggies, fruits, and berries on a daily basis. I have been taking this whole food product since 2009, and I know without any hesitation it should be included in everyone's diet. It is whole food fruits and vegetables that have been dehydrated in a cold process to preserve the nutritional quality, and put into vegetarian capsules. You can find more information about them here.

The most dramatic detox is Dr. Moritz's Ultimate Liver Cleanse. This is not for the faint of heart, but it does make a significant impact on how you feel. I recommend that you purchase the book and follow its guidelines closely. The program is intended to cleanse your liver and gallbladder of any stones that may be present within them, as the book describes, and it entails doing a variety of things like drinking apple juice for six days, followed by a regimen of epsom salts and a concoction of olive oil and grapefruit juice.

The detox that has reduced my general stiffness and inflammatory markers the most is Dr. Christopher's Shade Push-Catch Detox System. This system comes in a package as a one-month process at the least intense level, and a two-week process at the most intense level. This two-step liver cleanse process effectively "pushes" toxins to the gut and "catches" them with binders for safe, effective results, avoiding the problem that can happen with some detox systems where the toxins are pushed out of the liver and gallbladder, and then reabsorbed in the small intestine. This can lead to injury to the walls of the small intestine (leaky gut) and toxins permeating into the blood. Dr. Christopher's Shade program is easy to use and highly effective at reducing inflammation, and cleanses everything out of your body that is not supposed to be there.

The system that has had the greatest positive impact on my overall health involves mung beans. I recommend the Mung Bean Soup Detox found in the book Ancient Secrets of a Master Healer, by Dr. Clint G Rogers. At the time of this writing, I have participated in two separate 30-day mung bean soup detox challenges. Each one produced slightly different results, and both were highly effective. The first of these detoxes involved eating mung bean soup exclusively for seven days, and then adding various mild foods along with the mung bean soup for the remainder of the 30 days. Once I fully committed to doing it, I began to see the significant benefits, like improved texture of my skin, lowering abdominal pain, and losing four pounds the first day and a total of 13 pounds over the course of the 30 days. I have witnessed others losing more, possibly because they have more to lose. I got back down to my high school weight after losing 13 pounds. I enjoy mung bean soup so much, now that most days I have it for at least one meal, and I continue to witness subtle improvements in my health.

I recommend that you have an appointment with an Ayushakti doctor to assess your health via teleconference, and support you through your mung bean soup detox. At the time of this writing, these 30 -minute consults were just $20. To make an appointment, go here or call 1 800 280-0906.

Here is the recipe for Mung Bean Soup:

Dr. Naram's Marvelous Mung Bean Soup

This soup helps balance all 3 doshas (life elements), aids the clearing away of aam (toxicity) that gets logged in the body over time due to poor diet, lack of exercise, and living a sedentary lifestyle. Many of the ingredients may be purchased online or in Asian/Indian food stores.

Ingredients:

- 1 cup whole green dried mung beans, soaked overnight in water
- 4 cups water
- 1 tsp Himalayan or Rock Salt
- 1 Tb pure cow's ghee or sunflower oil
- 1 tsp black mustard seeds
- 2 pinches hing (called asafetida in the West)
- 1 bay leaf
- ½ tsp turmeric powder
- 1 tsp cumin powder
- 1 tsp coriander powder
- 1 pinch black pepper
- 1.5 tsp fresh ginger finely chopped
- ½-1 tsp, or 1 clove fresh garlic, finely chopped
- 3 pieces Kokum (dry jungle plum)
- Salt to taste when served.
- Optional: 1 cup chopped peeled carrots, 1 cup diced celery

Preparation:

1. Rinse, remove any debris, and then soak the mung beans in water overnight.

1. Drain the mung beans, put into a pressure cooker with all the remaining ingredients, adding the indicated amount of water and salt; then cook in a pressure cooker until tender. Usually around 25 minutes, until beans pop open.

1. Or, in a regular deep pot, bring beans to a boil, then put on low heat with the lid on or slightly cracked. Add kokum, carrots, and celery after 25 minutes. It will take 40-45 minutes for the beans to be fully cooked.

1. After the beans have been cooking for around 20 minutes, heat the oil or ghee in a separate small pot on medium heat until melted; add mustard seeds

1. When seeds start to pop, lower heat to lowest setting, add hing, bay leaf, turmeric, cumin, coriander, ginger, garlic, and black pepper, stir gently, mixing well. Simmer for 5-10 minutes; do not burn.

1. Transfer the seasoning mixture into the bean mixture, bring to a boil, then simmer for 10 more minutes.

1. Serve in soup bowls. May be served with basmati rice.

(Adapted from *Ancient Secrets of a Master Healer* (2020), by Dr. Clint G Rogers.)

If you have never used a detoxification program, you will be surprised at the shift toward greater health your body makes. My hope is you will initiate one of these programs right away, and watch your body and mind take on a new zest for life. Remember to consult with your doctor before doing this.

Chapter 5

What Are You Really Breathing?

Here we explore the importance of air quality and how you can make positive shifts in the air in your home and your environment.

If we live in a relatively smog-free, healthy environment, we don't spend time thinking much about air quality — until we need to. I will share methods to upgrade the air in your own home:

- Determine the quality of your indoor air.

- Change the filter in your furnace.

- Check/add other filters also.

- Keep your rugs and carpets clean.

- Control your home's humidity.

- Add plants.

There was a knock at the door. I was not expecting visitors. It was a vacuum cleaner salesman. I invited him in, his suitcase of information, vacuum, and a short R2-D2 looking thing. He said that the R2-D2 thing was an air filter, which he demonstrated.

I had been thinking about looking into air filters, without a known reason why. When the salesman, Nick, began his demonstration of the air filter, he first measured the particle count in my home. I wasn't familiar with this type of measurement system. He told me the particle count in my home was so high that he felt sure I had mold somewhere. I was pretty sure that I didn't have mold, and I had the delusional idea that I might smell it, or perhaps feel it or something. He had the testing equipment and showed me the results so I wasn't going to argue. The demonstration continued with him putting the Filter Queen Defender air filter in my bathroom with the door closed, where it ran for a while.

About 30 minutes later, it was amazing how much different the air smelled and felt. It seemed easier to breathe. I purchased two

Filter Queen Defender air filters that day. There is nothing more important than the quality of our air. I have run those two air filters in my home since then. I also put them in the bedrooms, so they protect my guests and myself when we sleep.

I had no idea how fortunate it was that I had these air filters until a few years later when, at the height of the recent pandemic, I discovered mold on two walls in my guest bedroom. I investigated further and found mold on the walls of three rooms, including my bedroom. It was hidden behind stacks of bookshelves and other furniture. There had been water damage in my home for a very long time that I couldn't see. This could have resulted in serious illness. I credit those filters for maintaining my health. They protected me at a time when I didn't have any idea that I needed protection.

The walls have now been fixed, the foundation cracks are repaired, and my home is dry, and I still run my filters. I even added an additional air filter. My air is always clean and the maintenance on these little, powerful machines is minimal and worth the investment. They seem to last forever with just filter replacements. They provide clean, high-frequency air continuously. And they may improve our health in subtle, yet powerful ways we are not even aware of.

Steps and Methods

The most common health symptoms of poor air quality are dryness and irritation of the eyes, nose, throat, and skin, headache, fatigue, shortness of breath, hypersensitivity and allergies, sinus congestion, coughing and sneezing, dizziness, and nausea. Of course, these symptoms can also be from other ailments, such as colds and flu, so it is unwise to use only health symptoms to determine if there are air quality issues.

Determine the quality of your indoor air.

First, purchase your own air quality monitor. There are currently quite a few indoor air quality monitors on the market that can effectively detect and even log over time the quality of the air inside your home. These devices typically check PM2.5 levels (tiny dust particles and other allergens in the air that you inhale), VOCs (Volatile Organic Compounds), temperature, and humidity, which are indicators for mold. According to Wikipedia, some of the most reliable air quality monitors on the market are the Foobot, Awair, Speck, and Air Mentor 6.

Second, check for signs and symptoms of mold. You can usually tell if there is a mold infestation in your home by using your eyes and your nose. My experience was apparently unusual. If you smell a musty odor coming from certain parts of your home, and cleaning doesn't remove the smell, you might want to consider hiring a professional for a mold test. Mold grows in moist areas like basements and dirty ductwork or drains. You can also look around for visible signs of mold, like growing black spots, water spots, or particularly damp areas in your home. These became evident at my home once the tall furniture was moved away from the walls.

Third, as a general rule, everyone should install smoke and carbon monoxide detectors in their homes. And because radon causes more fatalities annually than either of the others according to American Radon, LLC, it is wise to check for this as well. Though there are good detectors out there, it is best to use a test to determine radon levels in your home. This can be done by requesting a free test at American Radon LLC, 720-727-6826, or they can be purchased at home improvement stores.

Change your HVAC filter. When in doubt, it's always a good idea to change your air filters. You should change the air filters at least once every 90 days for the average family home. But if you suspect the air quality in your house is poor, such as after remodeling or house additions, you can change them more frequently. If you have a dog or cat in the house, you may need to change your air filters every 60 days or so. If anyone in your family has allergies, you should change the air filters more often; as often as every month is recommended

Don't forget about your other air filters. Home air filters come in a variety of qualities and prices. There are seven commonly used home air filter types: HEPA filters, ultraviolet air purifiers, activated carbon air purifiers, ionic air purifiers, electronic air cleaners, central air cleaners, and air-to-air exchangers. Each has their own uses, as well as pros and cons. Once you have made an investment in a home air filter, ensure they will work at their highest level of effectiveness by maintaining them regularly.

Keep your rugs and carpets clean. Many different pollutants can be held within the fibers of rugs and carpets. If dust and allergens are deeply embedded in your carpets, or circulating in the air throughout your home, allergy symptoms can elevate. Of course, frequent vacuuming and deep cleaning of your carpets will help to limit and remove many potential contaminants, leaving less to circulate in your air.

Control humidity in your home. Humidity is simply the amount of water vapor present in the air, and many things can cause these levels to fluctuate. When humidity is too high, mold and mildew can grow and reduce air quality. When humidity is too low, it facilitates the spread of infection, therefore compromising the immune system. More often than not, people do not measure and only realize humidity is too high once mold has already formed, or too low when static electricity becomes a problem, or the body tissues get dry. You can measure your humidity levels using a common humidity gauge, and ideal humidity for health and comfort is between 30% and 60%

Improve your air quality with indoor plants. Among the air quality benefits of indoor plants is fresh oxygen. Plants absorb carbon dioxide and release oxygen. Plants will also reduce contaminants because they absorb VOCs, especially when they are placed in the sun. Plants also metabolize toxins, removing the harmful effects they may harbor. Being around plants boosts our mental health by lowering the stress hormone cortisol, making the benefits of house plants particularly appealing for mental health support, as well.

Your Outdoor Air — Paradise or Poison?

Here, we explore the quality of our outdoor air. I will share two stories of air quality problems and how I have adjusted my life to avoid potential health risks. We will also share some practical ways you can easily improve the air quality in your neighborhood by employing the following techniques:

- Use organic lawn care products.

- Reduce auto emissions.

- Plant trees everywhere.

If you have a dog, or you like to go for walks or runs, you have probably passed by homes when they've recently used some kind of lawn treatment. The air is rife with chemicals, and it is dangerous to our health. There are many other air quality circumstances challenging our health, especially if you live in a place where there is a lot of traffic and industries.

I live in a relatively tree-filled neighborhood. It is easy to notice lawn treatments when I'm out for exercise or for walks with my dog. Sometimes I notice an odor creeping over from neighboring yards, as I'm sitting in my own yard. In our community, everybody has pristine lawns. Except me, because it goes against everything I believe in to use synthetic agents in order to fulfill a societal standard for beauty. I don't resist beauty, but when beauty is generated through chemical applications on the Earth and ultimately in the air, my dander rises. My animals and I walk and sit on the lawn. If we applied the standard yard chemicals, it would produce a significant risk to our health. When the animals clean themselves, the chemicals would get into their bodies and likely compromise their health and reduce their lifespan.

When out walking by a place where the smell of chemicals is prevalent, I pick up my dog and we hustle away to avoid the air and chemicals. I encourage you to do the same. While it is impossible to control what others do to their lawns, we can respond to the circumstances in a way that is safe for us. If you are a community leader, I hope you will make sure the air quality in your community is good. If you're not a community leader, and you have poor air quality, maybe it's your time to step up and into the role of being a community leader so that you can make an impact for the rest of the people around your home and around your community.

Steps and Methods

It must be on each and every one of us to do our part to take care of the air we breathe. Here are several ways to improve the macrocosm of our world:

Choose organic, chemical-free fertilizers and other products for your yard. Lawn chemicals can be absorbed through the skin, swallowed, or inhaled. As they are applied, lawn chemicals can drift and settle on ponds, laundry, toys, pools and furniture. Even pets are at risk. You can use organic treatments to give your lawn the food it needs, so weeds don't take up residency. I use many organic products from Sustane. There are organic lawn services that use natural products to support the beauty of your lawn.

Plant extra trees that help in cleaning up the outdoor air. In Japan, people save the pits from the fruit they eat and toss them out the windows in their cars, allowing nature to take care of the rest of the process. Trees in a community, in our yards, and throughout our community greatly improve the air we breathe in a variety of ways. Trees also remove pollutants from the air that could potentially contribute to health problems for residents. Gaseous pollutants such as ozone, carbon monoxide, nitrogen dioxide, and sulfur dioxide are absorbed into a tree through tiny openings in leaves (called stomata) and then are broken down within the tree. Trees provide other secondary benefits as well. Plant a tree, or a forest of trees, to improve the air quality all around you.

It is up to each of us to create healthy air quality in our communities. Let's all make a pact to do our part by no longer bending to the norms of society, which damage mother earth and the air we breathe.

Make Your Hot Air Work for You — Breathing Exercises

I met a breathing specialist more than 20 years ago and thought the profession was a bit weird, yet it made sense to me. Though I didn't follow the teachings at the time, eight years later I dove deep into Kriya meditation, which in Sanskrit is called pranayama, and in English means "breathing meditation."

Here, we will be addressing the importance of including an intentional breathing program in your healing process. I will share a story of my experience with Wim Hof breathing, and we will give you specific breathing routines that you can begin today, like the following:

- Belly Breathing

- Box Breathing

- Kriya Breathing meditations

Over the course of the past 11 years, I have been studying breathing exercises and breathing techniques. In the last year, I've learned a technique developed by Wim Hoff.

His techniques were the catalyst for a significant consciousness breakthrough. It has vital healing potential. Basic conscious breathing calms our mind and connects us to Source. Wim Hof techniques take it to the next level and can improve our health in significant ways.

My story begins in childhood. My father was having a 70-foot silo built on our farm property, when I was three years old. From the time that silo was beginning to be built ,it was my soul mission to climb all the way to the top. Like youngsters do, I repeatedly asked my dad to let me climb to the top. Dad was afraid of heights. He bargained with me by saying as soon as I could get to the ladder by myself, he would go to the top with me.

Since the ladder start at 12 feet off the ground and I was a tiny little 3-year-old, he thought he had negotiated a reprieve of at least a couple years, if not more. But I was focused on getting up that ladder. Within a very short time, possibly just two weeks, I had gotten myself up onto the ladder! And from a few rungs up the ladder, I shouted out to my dad, who was out in the cow lot not too far away, "Hey Dad, I'm on the ladder! Come on, let's go up!"

I can only imagine his internal reaction, but he shook his head in astonishment, shrugged his shoulders, and made his way to the ladder, ushering me toward my dream as he climbed over me and kept me between his hands and his feet as we ascended to the top. I was so excited.

This is one of my earliest memories, and I remember it in detail. We get to the top of the cylinder part of the silo, and Dad thinks I'm going to be satisfied because I'm at the top. But I said, "No, dad, I want to go up there," pointing to the top of the dome part of the silo. He is not sure what to do. So he says, "Okay, I'm going to crawl up as far as I can with you. And then you can stand on the top, and I'll hold onto your ankle. And that way everyone's safe."

I'm able to get up to the top. And when I'm standing at the top, I look out and I shriek, "Dad, this is so cool! You should come up here!" My memory is that I could see forever! I was experiencing the highest level of bliss at that moment. Dad was sure he was high enough and that he didn't need to come up any further.

I tell you all this so that you have a reference for the rest of the story. In a recent workshop, my coach was leading us in Wim Hoff breathing techniques, which is a series of breaths that are with a cadence. You do the cadence of really fast, hard breaths for 30 minutes. Then he guided us to use our intention to dredge up any energy from our bodies that shouldn't be there, starting from our feet, moving all the way up through our body and, as we got to our throat, we allow a gutteral, primal-sustained sound to emerge from our bodies, carrying with it the energy of whatever needed to be released.

I was feeling so good, I really had no idea there was anything to dredge up. Little did I know. After 30 minutes of intense breath work, we got to the point where we set our intention to dredge up all this energy, and our sound was to be caught by a pillow we held on our face. I thought to myself, "I'm not really sure what this is supposed to do, so I'll just do it as described." How surprised was I when I let out my yell into the pillow and huge amounts of emotion and huge amounts of past stories and pain that were stored deep within me came out with it.

First, my mind rolled through with one significant story, and then it rolled through with another significant story. And I was sobbing at the end of it, releasing this story that had been there for so long and had created an energy blockage within me that I didn't know was there. Then, lying in a heap, a visual came to my mind of my undamaged self standing gloriously on top of that silo, arms outstretched to God, receiving a full blast of love energy into my heart.

Behind me were faint images of all the hurt that I had been healing over all these years. It felt like my whole life had come full
circle from years of trauma, and then healing. And now the purest
representation of me had reemerged and put everything back to
that place where life could be experienced in its fullest and highest
vibration.

Breathing exercises can do this for you.

Steps and Methods

My breathing practice has become an invaluable part of my daily
routine. I use various techniques. I invite you to try them out and
develop your own daily practice.

Belly Breathing. The beginning of any breathing practice is returning back to our original breathing pattern. When we are born,
we automatically breathe all the way down into our bellies. Watch
the belly of a baby and you will see their little tummy rise and fall
with each breath. This is the most efficient way to breathe because our bodies are designed to use our diaphragm for drawing
in air. If you are not already naturally belly breathing, it is wise to
relearn this practice.

Do this by lying on the floor, placing one hand on your chest and
the other on your stomach. Consciously breathe into your stomach. Do this for two or three minutes each morning. It may take
some practice to reteach your diaphragm to expand when you
breathe, but it will eventually get the hang of it. Spend some time
every day practicing this technique. It will eventually become the
normal way you breathe. Until then, keep taking time out daily for
this practice.

Box Breathing. This is where you sit quietly, and, using belly breathing, you breathe in for four counts. Then hold for four
counts. Then breathe out for four counts. Then hold for four
counts. Repeat for five minutes. Expand your practice by increasing gradually from five minutes to 10 minutes, etc., up to 30 minutes or more.

Kriya Breathing and Meditation Techniques. My personal daily practice includes Kriya breathing. The most common style of Kriya breathing comes from Sudarshan Kriya from the ancient yogic science of India. "Su" means proper, and "darshan" means vision. "Kriya" in yogic science means to purify the body. As a whole, Sudarshan Kriya means "proper vision by purifying action."

After practicing Kriya for 16 years, I am qualified to teach these basic techniques:

1. Find a quiet place where you will not be disturbed or distracted.

2. Sit quietly with your spine straight sitting forward on the chair so your back is not supported.

3. Close your eyes and relax your body and mind, in preparation for a cleansing experience.

4. Say a prayer inviting the deity of your choice to be with you during this experience.

5. Begin the breathing process. Using your intention — breathe in through the bottom of your feet, bringing your breath all the up your body as Divine light, to the top of your head, and on the exhale, take the breath as Divine light down from the top of your head, all the way through your body, and out the bottom of your feet.

Repeat this many times maintaining your focus.

Wim Hof Breathing technique. Wim Hof has developed special breathing exertions that keep his body in optimal condition and in complete control in the most extreme conditions. The breathing technique is first and foremost premised on inhaling deeply, and exhaling without any use of force. Let's get started.

- Get comfortable

  Assume a meditation posture: sitting or lying down, whichever is most comfortable for you. Make sure you can expand your lungs freely without feeling any constriction. Do not attempt this standing up.

- 30-40 deep 2-step breaths

Close your eyes and settle in. Be conscious of your breath, and try to fully connect with it. Inhale deeply through the nose or mouth in a 2-step process, fully filling your stomach first, then filling your chest, and exhale unforced through the mouth. Repeat this 30 to 40 times in short, powerful bursts. You may experience light-headedness, and tingling sensations in your fingers and feet. These side effects are completely harmless.

- The hold

After the last exhalation, inhale one final time, as deeply as you can. Then let the air out and stop breathing. Hold as long as you can, until you feel you must breathe again.

- Recovery breath

When you feel you must breathe again, draw one big breath to fill your lungs. Feel your belly and chest expanding. When you are at full capacity, hold the breath for around 15 seconds, then let go. That completes round number one. This cycle can be repeated 3-4 times. After having completed the breathing exercise, take your time to bask in the bliss. This calm state is highly conducive to meditation, so allow yourself time for this.

Breathing techniques offer a myriad of healing possibilities for the mind and the body.

Chapter 6

Water and Life

Water is life, and we cannot take it for granted. We are made up mainly of water, but we don't give enough thought to the quality of the water we take in.

Most industrialized nations use chlorine and other harsh chemicals to make tap water free of parasites and bacteria that could cause sickness. In many communities, fluoride is added to the water supply to improve oral health.

We are mainly water. Everyone needs to drink it to live, and we must consume copious amounts to maintain good health.

As I was moving through my health journey, I had much to learn surrounding water and my health. Like most people, I drank tap water, and I swam in chlorinated swimming pools, and I poo-pooed drinking bottled water, which I still do. I did not realize the impact all of those things were having on me. When I had my tap water tested, I was mortified at the outcome of this test. It was being tested by a company that sells water filters so I did take that into consideration. And even so, if our bodies are made up of between 70% and 90% water, it makes sense that we want to put the highest quality water into them. And my water was far from that. I didn't realize the impact that tap water was having on my health until I started drinking purified water and spent more time researching what constitutes safe drinking water.

Currently, I have a Kangen water system, which filters out all impurities and leaves the good minerals. Though the system was an investment, I am getting significantly better water than I was getting before. I use that water for all eating and drinking needs, as well as for my plants and my animals. I also have filters on my showers that trap chlorine and some of the other contaminants. I stopped swimming in my chlorinated pool, and then I had it removed.

We need water to survive. Humans are made up of 70% water,

which is bound in our cell membranes. Water is more important than food – we can go up to a month without food, but can only survive a week without water. This makes it all the more crucial that we drink clean and pure water. Dehydration is the number one cause of stress in the human body. It has been linked with heartburn, headaches, angina pain, asthma, colitis, diabetes, peptic ulcer pain, high blood pressure, low back pain, blood cholesterol, and many other symptoms.

Steps and Methods

If you live in an industrialized country, you have some of the best water available. Unfortunately, there are still contaminants within the tap water that can lead to dangerous consequences if consumed over time. Here are some of them:

Chlorine: In the United States, chlorine has been a standard water additive since 1904. Adding chlorine in drinking water has done a good job of killing off most microorganisms. In fact, the United States has one of the safest water supplies in the world, and I am truly grateful for this. Without chlorine or some other form of water disinfection treatment, millions of people would die from devastating infections such as cholera, salmonella, and others.

Studies have shown that chlorine itself is not the main problem – it's when chlorine mixes with any type of organic matter in the water. In the 1970s, scientists discovered that when chlorine is added to water, it forms Trihalomethanes (THMs), one of which is chloroform. THMs increase the production of free radicals in the body and are highly carcinogenic.

Exposure to fluoride is a contentious topic, mostly because exposure is everywhere. Not only is fluoride a common ingredient in toothpaste, many municipalities have a fluoridated water supply. The reason we're given is that it encourages oral health, even though it's not known to prevent harmful oral bacteria. You may have positive associations with fluoride. You may envision tooth protection, strong bones, and an industry that cares about your dental needs.

What you may not know is that the fluoride added to drinking water and toothpaste is a crude industrial waste product of the aluminum and fertilizer industries, and a substance that is toxic enough to be used as rat poison. In short, fluoride is toxic. It affects the bones, it causes arthritis, it affects the thyroid, it calcifies the pineal gland, it accelerates female puberty, affects male fertility, damages the kidneys, and is harmful to the cardiovascular system.

There are many other contaminants found in our water supply that are hazardous to our health, including: lead, aluminum, chloramines, pharmaceuticals, mercury, volatile organic compounds (vocs), herbicides, pesticides.

The safest way to ensure that these toxins do not make it into your body is to have your water tested to determine which contaminants your tap water may contain. Once you have identified the contaminants present, you can select a water filtration solution that is best for you.

It is quite evident that drinking tap water is hazardous to your health. It is vital to take measures to filter the water you use for drinking and bathing to protect your health and your spiritual connection. I shared my story of learning how bad my own water was. We then provided deeply researched information warning about chemicals found in community water, the damage they create, and how to avoid them.

Water makes up the highest percentage of the human body. It is a well-known fact that we all need to keep our inner water tanks full. It is my belief we should be able to trust our water supply, yet it is proven that is not the case. My hope is that you have learned the importance of being vigilant of the water you use for drinking and bathing. By adding a whole house filter, or at least filters on all the high use water sources, you can experience greater health and, more importantly, make a more personal connection to the Source of all creation. Our water is an important connection to realizing our highest frequency.

Water Filtration

Here we will explore why pure water is so important. I will share my own story on how I made filtration decisions for my home, and I will give you the pros and cons of several options you can choose from, including:

- Whole house systems

- Faucet/shower systems

- Pour through systems

- Specialty Systems

There are many ways to improve your water quality. Some options are very reasonable in price, and some are very expensive. The important thing is, if you haven't already made this commitment to your health, now is the time to do it. The following information will give you a good foundation to make your water filtration system decisions.

Steps and Methods

If water is not treated, filtered, or purified, it can make you sick. Nowadays, we have advanced water technology, such as water filters and water filtration systems. Let's take a look at the benefits of water filtration and using water filters.

Filtered tap water is better than standard tap water and bottled water. Using water filters to filter tap water is much cheaper than buying bottled water, which is also not eco-friendly, due to the bottles' plastic production. Most bottled water actually comes from tap water, so you are really just paying for the plastic.

By purchasing a professional water filter, you will save yourself money, and you will be drinking higher quality water that has been filtered accordingly. Water filtration removes water impurities and dangerous contaminants such as chlorine, disinfection byproducts, and heavy metals such as mercury, lead, and arsenic. At the same time, water filters ensure that important minerals such as magnesium, calcium, and zinc are retained. They protect you from toxins and ensure that you consume healthy minerals.

Whole-house filtering system. A whole-house filter has a number of benefits. The greatest benefit is that wherever you are using your water, it has the same quality of filtering. You do not have to worry about the children using the wrong sink for drinking water, for example. Another benefit is that you have just one location where filters need to be replaced. There are whole house filters available that will remove whatever contaminant you need to remove. They vary in price between $500 and $10,000, and it is recommended to have a trained professional install them.

Pros and cons of faucet/shower systems. These filters fit right onto your faucet. You remove the aerator and put the filter onto the tap. The tap water filter then removes the impurities from the water and dispenses clean water for you to drink. With water faucet filters, you are able to switch between filtered and unfiltered water. So if you need water to cook or drink you can turn on the filter and if you are washing dishes, you leave it off. This type of water filtration is effective, efficient, decently priced, and very easy to install. Among disadvantages: They do tend to slow down your water flow. Like all water filtration systems, these require replacement, and some of the latest models come with digital indicators that tell you when it is time to replace a filter.

Pros and cons to pour-through systems. There are many of these options at many price points. Advantages include portability and effectiveness at removing contaminants. There are currently 2-step filters, and 5-step filters on the market. The 5-step filters provide more-pure water after filtering, and they are also typically more expensive to purchase and to maintain.

Pros and cons to specialty systems like Kangen. The Japan-based company has been the leading manufacturer of alkaline ionizers and water filtration machines in the world for over four decades. Kangen Water® is delicious water created from their innovative water technology. These devices filter your tap water, and they also produce ionized alkaline and acidic waters through electrolysis. These waters can be used for various purposes, including drinking, cooking, beauty, and cleaning.

My hope is that this information will provide you the foundational and detailed information to help you make your water filtration decisions.

Quantity of Water We Drink

It's important to drink water, so how much should we be drinking? Conflicting information can be confusing.

I will share my own story related to dehydration, and I will delineate the following important considerations to use when determining how much water you should really drink:

- What is the right amount?

- What counts in the equation?

- Health conditions that affect the amount

Dehydration is a health problem worldwide. Medicaldaily.com reports that up to 75% of the American population is chronically dehydrated. In countries where water is abundant, this may not make sense, yet it is the reality. My hope is you will recognize your own circumstances and make the changes necessary to keep your body's water tank at the optimum level for excellent health.

It was often sort of a bragging point that I rarely had to drink water. In fact, there were times in my life when I was drinking only the water that I drank after I brushed my teeth in the morning, without adding any further water throughout the day. I don't know why I didn't feel poorly because I was surely dehydrated. Maybe I just didn't understand that I was feeling poorly, but I have increased my water intake significantly over the course of time — and quantity does matter.

We often hear people need to drink eight glasses of water a day. That's a standard number. Or another concept is people should drink half their body weight in ounces each day to be certain they're getting enough water on any given day. That may be true, but it also may not be true, depending on the circumstances.

My water intake clearly was not enough. I had dramatic symptoms of dehydration. My lips were always dry. My ears were flaky and dry. The skin on my lower legs I referred to as alligator skin, rough and scaly, not just dusty, but crunchy. Sometimes I would get cracks in the sides of my fingers from my system being so dry. I would get cuticle damage from hangnails that would hurt and bleed. When I started increasing the quantity of my water intake, all of those symptoms went away.

My water experience has been a bit of a learning curve, but now I have done the work to get it turned completely around. You too can improve your health and your connection to Source by drinking a higher quality of water and a greater quantity of water.

Steps and Methods

Should everyone drink 6-8 glasses of water a day? Everyone needs water for every single body function. It flushes toxins from your organs, carries nutrients to your cells, cushions your joints, and helps you digest the food you eat. If you don't get enough water, you can become dehydrated. Dehydration is the number one cause of stress in the human body. It has been linked with heartburn, headaches, angina pain, asthma, colitis, diabetes, peptic ulcer pain, high blood pressure, low back pain, blood cholesterol, and many other symptoms. That's why it's important to get the water your body needs every day.

No set amount is right for everyone. How much you need can depend on your size, how much you exercise, how hot the weather is, the perspiration you produce, how well the water you drink is being absorbed, among other things. With those things in mind, it is recommended by ancient Ayurvedic medicine to drink 8-10 cups daily, and adding to that if you are exercising vigorously or working in the heat, taking into consideration the amount of perspiration that is normal for you.

What counts in the equation? Your recommended water intake includes all sources, drinking water, other beverages, and food. But be careful — certain fluids have their drawbacks. For instance, juices, sodas, and smoothies can be hydrating, but they can also be high in sugar and calories. Coffee and tea provide water, too. But, they also contain caffeine, which can make you lose more water through elimination. Most healthy people can safely drink two to four 8-ounce cups of coffee each day. Scale back if it makes you feel anxious or jittery.

Alcoholic drinks contain water, too. But like caffeine, they actually cause you to lose more water through your urine. This can lead to dehydration.

Sports drinks have a high water content. They also contain carbohydrates and electrolytes, which can help you absorb water and keep your energy levels up. During intense workouts, they help to replace salt lost through sweat. But be careful: Many also contain lots of extra calories, sugar, salt, synthetic ingredients, and food dyes. Check the nutrition label. Pay attention to the serving size, and limit how many you drink, if any.

Energy drinks are different from sports drinks. They contain sugar, as well as stimulants, like caffeine, often in high doses. Many doctors recommend that children and teens avoid them. I recommend no one drink them. My athletes used to drink them at half time in their sports contests. It was one of my biggest irritants, because I was trying to keep them hydrated for peak performance, and it was nearly impossible when that much stimulation was in their systems.

We get hydration from the food we eat, also. Fruits and vegetables like cucumbers, iceberg lettuce, celery, and watermelon are over 90% water. They also provide a variety of different vitamins and minerals. This is where I get much of my water intake, and because they are from nature, the body absorbs them quite well.

I Drink but I'm Still Dry: Absorption

Here, we will dive into how to be certain the water you are taking in is absorbed. I will share a story of my own experience with hydration and that of the athletes I worked with in the sports medicine arena and give you information about these tips and tricks to ensure you are receiving benefits from the water you are taking in:

- Drink only warm water.

- Structure your water.

- Bless your water.

- Program your water.

Sometimes, though, people may drink a lot but not absorb water properly. I had this problem. I would increase my water intake and would have to make frequent runs to the bathroom. My productivity was diminishing as a result.

Our bodies are like potted plants. When you have a very dry plant and you pour water in it, it runs through the edges of the pot because the dirt is really dry and doesn't readily absorb the water. If you keep putting a little water in at a time, though, the dirt absorbs the water and then it stays in the pot.

We need to keep our bodies hydrated so that they will absorb the water, but there are other mechanisms by which we can assist in helping the water absorb. When I employed these techniques, my bathroom runs were fewer, and everything seemed to work better. My water absorption is now so high that even if I drink an eight- or 16-ounce glass of water right before going to bed at night, it's normal to sleep through the night without a middle-of-the-night bathroom run.

Steps and Methods

Here are some of the tips and tricks I have learned that can increase absorption of the water you drink:

Drink only warm water, because it absorbs much better than cold water. Warm water also increases the heat, the agni, the digestive fire inside of your abdomen throughout your digestive system. To remain hydrated in the easiest way, drink smaller amounts throughout the day. Drinking large volumes at any given time is not as beneficial as drinking small amounts regularly during the day.

Structured water is healthier and absorbs better than unstructured water. I encourage you to structure your water in some way. Structured water is essentially putting your water into a vortex like a tornado for a short period of time. This groups the molecules into smaller, more easily absorbed clusters. When the molecules of the water are smaller, they are able to get into the cells easier. When they are able to get into the cells, they, in turn, are not passing through the kidneys as quickly.

If the kidneys are letting the water pass through pretty quickly, that could indicate an issue with the kidneys. It could also indicate an issue with absorption of the water. Reducing the size of the molecules of your water through structuring creates a much healthier water option and is relatively easy to accomplish.

Here are two easy ways to structure the water you drink:

- Fill a heavy kettle with water and boil it on the stove for a minimum of 10 minutes. Longer is better. This adds extra oxygen into the water and improves the absorption.

- Using two empty 2-liter pop bottles, glue the two lids together back to back and drill a ½-inch hole in the tops, so the threads of the lids are undamaged, but there is a hole all the way through, creating a lumpy cylinder. Next, fill one bottle with clean, filtered water. Screw the one side of the cap onto the filled water. Then screw the empty bottle onto the other side of the lid. Be certain the lids are tight, and flip the bottles over so the empty one is on bottom and the full one is one top. Watch the water spin out of the full bottle, creating a vortex as it flows into the bottom bottle. Drink the water out of the now full bottle of structured water.

In the picture below, which illustrates the water-structuring process, notice the vortex in the upper water bottle.

Vortex in water of upper bottle

Put a blessing on your water. In his book, Hidden Messages in Water, Massaro Emoto wrote about how the environment influences water. When the positive emotions of love and gratitude were shown to water, the crystal structure was beautifully formed. When the water was shown negative emotions of hatred, deformed and ugly water crystals developed. Bless your water with positive prayers, and tape loving positive words to the pipes that enter your home, and those in the bottom of your kitchen sink for an extra boost of goodness for the water that gets into your food.

Chapter 7

Fitness and Spiritual Connection

A lot of people made jokes about gaining "Covid-19 fat" during the pandemic, when a lot of people put on weight due to isolation, stay-at-home orders, and a general lack of motivation and bodily movement. I myself failed to participate in much physical activity, and I also ate less healthily than ever before. Like many of us, I gained weight, too.

This gave me perspective on other people's struggles — but it also motivated me to share what I knew with others. You see, physical fitness isn't just cosmetic. It affects our entire being. Physical fitness affects not only our general perspective of our body, but it also affects our feeling of connection to our highest self, our Source. When we are physically fit, we are more deeply connected to Source.

Here, we will explore aligning your physical and spiritual bodies together with a unique twist on the reasons for fitness. I will share my personal story of allowing my body and spirit to fall out of alignment, and I will offer tips for getting more connected to your body as a spiritual being:

- Your body is in service to you.

- Exercise is a form of spiritual connection.

- Love yourself through exercise.

- Step beyond your comfort zone.

- Exercise stabilizes emotional energy.

- Connect to sacred breath.

During the recent year of pandemic-related isolation, I gained a whole new perspective on the physical aspects of my life. I have almost always been fit, and fitness played a significant role throughout my life, but during 2020 that was not the case. I realize now that the worldwide energy was deeply oppressive. It permeated everyone's heart and mind with sorrow, worry, and low-frequency energies. My lifestyle patterns reflected the low frequency influence of the whole world.

I neglected to do much physical activity and ate less healthfully. For the first time in my life, I gained weight, about 10 pounds. While it gave me perspective related to other people's struggles, it also made me feel out of control, with a lower sense of my physical self. I had to get hold of myself. I was able to gain back much of what I lost with regard to strength, flexibility, personal perspective, and also my normal body size. How we feel when our physical body is not in a comfortable level of fitness has a direct effect on our state of mind. As the pandemic began to subside, I was able to gain back the physical abilities I had before, as well as my feeling of connection. Isn't that what we're all here for?

Bruce Tainio of Tainio Technology invented and built a machine called a BT3 Frequency Monitoring System, an accurate sensor to measure bio-electrical frequencies of plant nutrients, foods, and even thoughts. As intriguing as Tainio's research is, its foundation may have been inspired by research done in the early years of the 20th century by Dr. Royal R. Rife, M.D. (1888-1971). Dr. Rife conducted research with a machine he developed called a "frequency generator" that applies currents of specific frequencies to the body. He concluded that every disease has a specific frequency.

According to Dr. Rife, every cell, tissue, and organ has its own vibratory resonance. Working with his frequency generator, he found that specific frequencies would destroy a cancer cell or a virus. His research demonstrated that certain frequencies could prevent the development of disease, and that others would neutralize disease. This is foundational information for understanding our health.

According to Dr. Tainio's research, a normal healthy body resonates at a frequency of 62-68 MHz. If the MHz drops to 58, health begins to deteriorate. Flu sets in at 57. If the MHz drops to 55, major health challenges set in, and cancer can set up shop at 42.

Additional interesting information regarding the body from Dr. Tainio's research:

- Brain frequency of a genius: 80-82 MHz

- Normal brain frequency: 72-78 MHz

- Human body frequency (excluding head): 62-28 MHz

- Thyroid and parathyroid glands: 62-68 MHz

- Heart: 67-70 MHz

- Lung: 58-65 MHz

- Liver: 55-60 MHz

- Pancreas: 60-80 MHz

- Colds and Flu: 57-60 MHz

- Candida growth: 55 MHz

- Receptive for viruses: 52 MHz

- Receptive to cancer: 42 MHz

- Death starts: 25 MHz

When we do what is necessary to maintain physical health, we find our minds are sharper and better able to think, remember, learn, and focus. The need for a sharp mind is just as important for spiritual matters as physical!

But our world is filled with opportunities for us to abuse our bodies. Many of the typical "fast foods" are quite limited in important vitamins and minerals and are instead filled with fats, sugars, and chemicals that actually destroy good health.

Steps and Methods

Here are ways to treat your body as a temple:

Use your body for greater happiness and fulfillment. Even though we are spiritual beings having a physical experience, and not the other way around, our bodies are the means by which we are able to remain alive on this earth plane. Your body's here to serve you as your living space on this planet. You cannot live here without it. And, if you treat it like a temple for the spiritual YOU that you are, it will serve your living needs in a beautiful, harmonic way.

If you treat it like a storage unit, throwing things into it without caution, and letting it be unkempt and disheveled, it will fall apart early, and you will have to transition into your next circle of life, perhaps in an untimely way. As we come closer and closer to aligning with our fullest spiritual connection, our body aligns with that high frequency connection and becomes more and more healthy.

Use your fitness time as a time to honor your body and reflect. Taking time to honor your body will improve your connection to the temple it is intended to be. When we engage our body with moderate activity, it responds by improving our health in many ways beyond muscles and bones. During the activity you choose, thank your body for its ability to do whatever you are engaged in. Ask your body what else it would like to have you do. Listen to it.

Engage your heart. Taking care of your physical body is a demonstration of love for yourself. If we look at exercise and good nutrition as a chore that we have to do, it will not serve our bodies in the highest way. If we look at exercise and nutrition as something we want to do to serve our body because of all it does for us, that will manifest overall health in a greater way. Being in joy during your activities is optimal. Joy opens the heart, and an open heart heals all things.

Expand your comfort zone. Once we engage in something new and learn the activity, we begin to develop a new level of comfort with it, and often it helps us overcome stored fears we may hold within us. It is an opportunity to step past the walls of your comfort into a new horizon, where you get to shine even brighter.

Release emotion and energy. This is one of the top reasons for engaging your body in activity. It turns out we are an amalgamation of all the emotions of generations before us, some say for at least seven generations. Exercise assists in releasing these emotions by twisting and compressing and stretching the muscles, joints, and organs where those emotions are stored. That was and is one of the main reasons for the asanas (movement and stretching) in the ancient science of yoga.

Take a moment to breathe. Breathing is always sacred. It is the difference between being alive in our bodies, and no longer being here on this Earth. Everytime we breathe, we take in the Divine breath from the Source that keeps us living on this earth plane. Having this intention during activities is the most sacred way to exercise.

Maintaining an elevated body frequency will ensure that your body can hold an elevated spiritual frequency and allow your body to be in service to you as you perform your personal mission during your life on earth.

Balance

Having an ability to balance is not a focus in many forms of fitness, but it's a significant aspect of health. The reason elderly people have to begin using canes and walkers is due to balance. And our body's balance is a reflection of having balance in many other areas of life.

Here, we will explore reasons for maintaining exceptional balance. I will share my handstand story, and will describe the following balance activities you can use to upgrade your own balance:

- Flamingo

- Dancer

- Figure 4

- Airplane

As you step up your practice with these balance activities, my hope is you will continue to add more and more difficult balance moves to your daily routine.

Handstands have been my barometer for my physical health. I continued to do handstands after many years in gymnastics as a child and young adult, through college. I did fewer of them during the isolation in 2020. I don't really have the space at my home to practice handstands, and so I didn't. I was pretty amazed that my strength diminished measurably over the course of that year, to the point where I no longer felt safe to be upside down on my hands. This was a giant shift in my perspective, because I have always done handstands.

When life was getting back to a new state of normal as the pandemic was winding down, parts of the world began to return to gyms and restaurants and move around in the community. I started walking, doing strength training, and doing yoga. Each day after my yoga class, I walked up to a wall and kicked into a handstand against the wall. And then I held it for a while. It didn't take very long to regain the ability to handstand in the middle of the room. And it made such a difference in the way I felt about myself and life.

Balance in our physical bodies depicts balance in so many other areas of our life. It depicts our balance emotionally. It depicts our balance mentally. It even depicts our balance with regard to our digestion and our level of toxicity in our bodies. So when our physical bodies are able to balance and be graceful and move with ease, then all of that is a reflection on other parts of our body and our life as well. Elderly people who have not maintained an active lifestyle initially lose strength, then their flexibility diminishes, and eventually their balance goes, and they have to use a cane or a walker to get around.

My Mom is one of those people. I was unwilling to watch my Mom deteriorate as long as she was a willing participant. She has always been relatively active, and as she got into her 80s her knees bothered her, so she gradually stopped doing many of the activities that kept her body strong and mobile. And then she began to fall quite easily. One day I saw her go down and knew why. Her hip strength was not strong enough to catch her when her gait was interrupted by a rock, garden hose, or crack in the sidewalk. I showed her some basic balance activities and she did them. After just two weeks, she felt more secure on her feet, and she has not fallen in several months. I continue to encourage her to upgrade her balance exercises. Doing those alone will increase her strength in the muscles around her hips and dramatically improve her confidence on her feet.

Steps and Methods

Here are some activities I showed her that you can do, too:

Exercise one: Basic "Flamingo" balance for people with difficulty walking. Place two high-backed chairs back-to -back, three to 4 ft. apart. These are your assistants. Stand between them with your arms spread out and your hands hovering over the backs of the chairs without touching. Lift one foot off the floor by bending your knee. Be certain to keep your hips at equal heights, not letting the hip of the lifted leg drop. Focus your eyes on the wall in front of you or on a spot on the floor 5 ft. or more in front of you. Hold this position without touching your hands to the chair for as long as you can. Repeat this activity 5 times on the first leg before switching to the other leg. Repeat this activity 2 tlmes daily.

Exercise two: Each of the following exercises will graduate in difficulty to accommodate increasing levels of practice. This "Dancer" exercise is similar to the first. Stand between the chairs with your hands hovering over the backs of the chairs, but not touching. Instead of bending the knee to lift the foot off the floor, this time you lift the whole leg backwards using your buttocks muscles until your foot is a few inches off the floor. Again, focus your eyes on one spot on the wall or floor. Hold for as long as you can without grabbing the chair with your hand or hands. If you need to touch the chair to aid in your balance, that is why they are there. Avoid holding on, though. Attempt this movement 5 times before switching to the other leg. With each attempt, you can time yourself to see how long you can hold it. You will notice over a short period of time you can easily hold this position longer and longer.

The "Figure 4" exercise. Again in the same starting position, turn your knee out to the side and place the bottom of that same foot on your ankle (easiest), your calf, (medium) or your inner thigh (harder). Again focus your eyes on one spot on the wall or floor. Hold that position using the backs of the chairs to assist you, only as you absolutely need to. Attempt this 5 times before switching to the other leg. With each attempt, you can time yourself to see how long you can hold it. You will notice over a short period of time you can easily hold this position longer and longer

The "Superman" or "Airplane." This time put one of your chairs in front of you about 3 feet, with the back toward you. Start with your hands on the back of the chair and one of your legs lifted into the "Dancer" position. Now bend forward at the supporting hip until your body is almost parallel to the floor. Remember to focus your eyes on one spot. Touch your hands on the back of the chair as needed, eventually lifting your hands away from the back of the chair. Holding your hands up above the chair is "Superman." When you are able to balance well enough in this position and you are comfortable taking your hands away from the chair, you can move your arms into a "T" position and hold without your assistant. This is called "Airplane." Try this 3 times before switching to the other leg. With each attempt you can time yourself to see how long you can hold it. You will notice over a short period of time you can easily hold this position longer and longer, as well.

When you are comfortable with each of these exercises using the chairs to assist, you can add a soft surface to stand on, like a foam mat or a pillow, and attempt all the exercises again.

These will give you a good start in improving your balance. As you become more accomplished, I encourage you to join a basic yoga class to advance your abilities.

It is never too late to get started. Let's get you started today.

Flexibility

Very few people spend time improving their flexibility, even though the benefits are vast, and flexibility enables the body to flow when you move. A few people are blessed with natural flexibility, but most of us must work at it to gain freedom of movement. Perhaps the reason most people don't focus on it is because the benefits are unknown and there are limited fitness practices that focus on it.

Here, we will explore flexibility as it relates to your overall health. I will share my story of having a rigid mind that resulted in a frozen shoulder, and I'll provide you with a list of the surprising benefits of gaining flexibility in the following categories:

- the physical benefits

- the spiritual benefits

- the emotional benefits

- the psychological benefits

Several years ago when I was still in my former job, I knew that I had gotten to a place in my life where I was questioning whether or not I should continue working there. It had been 26 years, and though I really loved my work, I kept getting nudges that there was something else I should be doing. I was having an inner dialogue with regard to my satisfaction in my work, what I was planning for and how I should be moving forward.

As a result of being stuck in life, my body began to demonstrate signs of being stuck. I started developing a frozen shoulder. I noticed a stiffness while I was doing a handstand. I could feel that my shoulder would not open far enough to get up into the position comfortably. I also noticed I couldn't bend over to touch my toes as easily as before. In fact, I could barely bend over and reach my shins. Over the course of the next six to eight months, my shoulder got progressively more limited in range, to the point where I could not lift my arm up to 90 degrees in any direction, despite being a sports medicine professional knowing and doing all the exercises necessary for proper therapy. Daily rehab was not improving the situation.

A surgical procedure became necessary because my work — which was taking care of the rehabilitation needs of injured athletes — required the use of my arm. It was my dominant arm, and the level of pain was a constant 7 out of 10. The surgery was performed in time for the next football season. Unfortunately, even after surgery the pain remained. I struggled at work wearing a sling and continuing my own therapy.

To maintain my fitness, I tried zumba (Latin American physical fitness routine) and other fitness classes, yet I wasn't able to do much. I started taking yoga for the first time in my life. It was slower paced, and I could adapt the movements to my abilities. My inner dialog during those classes was a comedy routine. Each time the instructor demonstrated a move, my inner ranting would begin: "What on earth! No one can do that move! Never mind me with one arm! I'm dying here!" This dialog, though internally expressed, went on nonstop. But through those yoga classes (over the course of the next month and a half to two months), I regained all of my shoulder range of motion, and the pain completely went away.

As I gained physical flexibility, it opened up my connection with Source even more. Our bodies will demonstrate our connection or lack of connection to our spiritual self through pain and immobility.

So my rigid body was a demonstration of rigidity in my thinking. I invite you to work on increasing your range of motion in your physical body, and thereby increase your flexibility in life, generally.

After many years of gymnastics, I was highly flexible, able to move my limbs in nearly any direction without limitation. Splits all three ways, back bends grabbing my ankles, laying down on my outstretched straight legs completely flat. I remember often watching television lying on my back, my butt pushed up next to the middle of the couch, with my legs stretched out in opposite directions and my heels hooked under either end of the bottom of the couch. At the time, I thought it was relatively normal. After college, my gymnastics career ended, and I began lifting weights and bodybuilding competitively. Weightlifting does not enhance your flexibility. In fact, it reduces it. So the limber body I once had was replaced by a highly muscular, inflexible body.

Steps and Methods

Over the course of time, I have realized how flexibility has so many benefits beyond the physical ones. I will present some of them here (I credit the site The Genius of Flexibility for some of this brilliant information):

The physical benefits of stretching. Astounding physical and physiological changes result from developing greater flexibility. As you follow a regular stretching or yoga routine, you will experience more fluidity in your movements. Soon you will be sitting up straighter, you will be feeling lighter in your step, and you will be walking taller. Flexibility makes you more youthful and childlike in your movements and more confident in the way you move. Stretching will also enhance your power, strength, and endurance. Another benefit is that often, chronic pain will disappear.

The spiritual benefits of stretching. Becoming more flexible connects you with positive life changes while it disconnects you from objectionable parts of your life. Changes in awareness and modifications in perspective become daily occurrences. You will find yourself showing greater integrity and enjoying doing the things that are good for you. You will begin to live more and suffer less. You will feel a greater connection to energy and spirit, and you will enjoy living with more grace.

Flexibility is a reflection of your life. Stretching allows you to experience a state of interconnec- tedness. It can provide you with a feeling of oneness with all of life. It brings about a connection to powers greater than yourself. Flexibility opens you to new awareness and perspectives.

The emotional benefits of stretching. Exciting emotional changes result from developing greater flexibility. Stretching and twisting our bodies aid in "wringing" out stored emotions that are held within. The emotional benefits are vast and will continue to unfold over time. They are present and working for you in a positive way.

The psychological benefits of stretching. Dramatic psychological changes can result from developing greater flexibility. Stretching allows you to experience greater self-acceptance, which allows your true personality to shine. Trusting yourself makes you better at decision-making, self-expression, and even more trusting of others. Stretching helps you to be available to greater levels of understanding, and humor.

Chapter 8

The Frequency of Words

Words are extremely powerful tools that we can use to uplift our personal energy and improve our lives, though we're often not conscious of the words we speak, read, and expose ourselves to. Even the words of others can easily affect our personal vibration. If you spend a few minutes with a chronic complainer who uses all sorts of negative terms, you'll feel your personal energy bottom out. Words have great power, so we must choose them (and our friends) wisely.

When Doreen Virtue and her son Grant were recording podcasts, they noticed that whenever she said the word angel, the recording graphics were shaped like angel wings! So they studied other words and realized that those with a spiritual or loving basis had large graphs and conversely negative words created graphs that were tight and small.

Here we will explore the impact of the frequency of the words you use. I will provide impressive reasons in the following ways to upgrade your use and exposure to words.

- Positive words produce positive vibrations.

- Negative words produce negative vibrations.

- Even your intentions influence the frequency.

- Make your words work for you.

You'll come to understand why positive words express the most energy and therefore have the most power to manifest your dreams. You'll also see how negative words have low energy and how they can actually draw negative experiences to you.

For many years, I was the program director concerning injury care and therapy for athletes at a private collegiate institution. I implemented certain rules to keep a sports medicine operation running smoothly. One was that everyone who used the facility would watch their language and make a concerted effort to not use swear words. In fact, I initiated a swear jar, where whenever anyone used a swear word, in particular the "F-bomb," they owed the jar a quarter. We did have some exceptions to the rule, for example, if someone sustained a traumatic injury or if an athlete's rehab was particularly painful, they were allowed a handful of undisciplined swear words. But general swearing in everyday language was frowned upon, called out, and fined.

At the time, I had no real reason to prevent this from happening besides believing that these kids were in college to expand their lives, and in my mind they needed to be more creative in the language they used rather than to mindlessly insert three "F-bombs" in every sentence. It was more about helping the student athletes recognize the language they used. I have to admit, swear words were never used in my house while I was growing up, and they did feel offensive to me, but that wasn't the reason I implemented the rule. At least, so I thought.

Steps and Methods

Words are extremely powerful tools that we can use to uplift our personal energy and improve our lives, though we're often not conscious of the words we speak, read, and expose ourselves to. Yes, even the words of others can easily affect our personal vibration. Spend a few minutes with a chronic complainer who uses all sorts of negative terms, and you'll feel your personal energy bottom out. Words have great power, so choose them (and your friends) wisely.

Positive words produce positive vibrations and positive sensations, and bring about positive thoughts and positive life outcomes. Words are often used without a thought, but a deeper look at your choice of words can either make or break your business, finances, relationships, and career. Doreen Virtue's book Angel Words powerfully illustrates this. She describes a volt meter that measures the frequency of words, the potential effect of words on our bodies, and the atmosphere around us. This voltmeter shows that the words we speak have a frequency impact on us and on the environment we are surrounded by. Words hold either a positive, neutral, or negative frequency.

Doreen Virtue and her son used the voltmeter to demonstrate the difference between a high-frequency utterance and a low-frequency utterance through a picture of a jagged frequency versus a more smooth frequency, and a higher peak vs a lower one.

It makes sense that the words we speak, think, and hear from others have a frequency effect on our bodies. So if we choose to use negative, low-frequency words, our bodies feel that and respond in an unfavorable way, over time causing a toll on our health. The opposite is true, too.

When we use elevated words that hold a high frequency, our cells also feel that and respond in a positive, life-enhancing way. Elevated frequency words are words that depict happy, loving ideas like gratitude, kindness, love, and generosity. And, of course, there are many others, but the effect is huge. Positive words are an investment that costs nothing, yet which yield very high dividends. Just the mere act of altering your vocabulary and using life-affirming words can dramatically and quickly change your life in magical ways.

Negative words produce negative vibrations and negative sensations, and bring about negative thought patterns and negative life outcomes. When we use low-frequency words such as swear words, the entire environment around us drops in frequency, including our cells. Swear words are not the only low-frequency words. Others that depict low-frequency ideas such as hate, frustration, anger, and jealousy are examples of words that will produce a negative impact on us.

What words are you using in your life, to criticize yourself, your life, or others? Replace any words that aren't of high frequency with positive words. Essentially, it's the idea of saying what you do want instead of what you don't want. There are many ways we manifest in our lives, and our words and thoughts are very powerful manifestation frequencies.

What about the intention behind our words? Have you ever noticed any unpleasant reactions whenever you or others around you engage in negative discussions? No matter how juicy the gossip, if you really pay attention, it is possible to feel your stomach tightening or experience other negative sensations in response to talking about low-frequency topics.

Gossip is definitely low frequency, and creates a vibrational ripple into the world, affecting everyone in its path, including the people you are talking about. Have you heard the concept that the lowest form of conversation is talking about others? Unfortunately, the same holds true with what we listen to on television or other media. Listening to the news is an invitation to lower your own energy field, and the energy field in your entire environment. When the frequency of your environment is perpetually low, it has a negative effect on the way you feel physically, as well as your level of happiness.

If we're not fully conscious of what we're exposing ourselves to, catching yourself consistently will eventually lead to success. Consider how many times you have called yourself stupid, untalented, ugly, or anything else, whether out loud or in your mind, and you may understand how your own words can shape a false self-image. The following are some strategies for improving the word vibrations in your life:

- Make words work for you. Consciously gain control over your own use of words. This is the best place to start.

- Don't judge others or yourself. Everyone is doing the best they can at any moment in time with the consciousness they have to work with, including you. Be kind and offer yourself the same empathy and compassion you would extend to anyone else.

- Stop self-deprecation. Never make your body, your creations, or anything else in your life the bad side of a joke. Words have power, and, unfortunately, the quantum field doesn't understand your sense of humor.

- Resist gossiping and speaking ill of others. Your words resonate through you, as well as through others.

- Go on a "negativity" diet. When you hear yourself thinking or saying something negative, correct it right away. Eventually your choices will only be positive expressions.

- Boost the positive energy of words. Everyone loves enthusiasm. Instead of expressing that you like what someone is wearing, say something like, "What you are wearing is absolutely stunning!" This feels much better and generates a bigger energetic response in the body.

- If you have negative people in your circle of friends, limit the time you spend with them, while you find higher frequency friends. As we have discussed, negative energy has a way of draining the energy of everything surrounding it. Avoid it when you can.

- Surround yourself with positive, uplifting words. Put affirmations on sticky notes around your home and office that say wonderful things about you, your family, or your goals. Wear clothes that have positive messages or phrases on them. Imagine the kind of positive energy you'll be generating for yourself when you're wearing positivity all day long. As you keep doing these things, you use the power of repetition in a highly effective way for your benefit. You have the power to change your world, and using words consciously is one of the quickest ways to shift the energy you bring into your life.

My hope is you are already motivated to upgrade your own language so as to upgrade what you bring to yourself, which will positively influence the life you and those around you live.

Does this information resonate with you? Are you ready to elevate the frequency of your language?

The Intention of Statements

The second aspect of the Eightfold Path of Buddhism is Right Intention or Right Thought. The Vietnamese Zen teacher, Thich Nhat Hanh, offers meaningful practices for Right Intention or Right Thinking. Why are thoughts and intentions so important? This is an intense area to investigate for all of us.

Here, we are exploring how to discover your deepest intentions. I will share my story of the unexpected outcome of my Mom's intention, and we will explore ways such as those listed below to uncover our deepest intentions:

- Go deep within; the source of intention may be in your pain.

- Be vigilant with your inner healing.

- Feel into the emotions of your words.

- Choose your idioms wisely.

I use sound healing in my healing clinic for my clients. One Thanksgiving a while ago at my home, my family and I were playing my Tibetan healing bowls, my alchemy bowls, and my crystal bowls, and we were creating a symphony of sounds in my home. My Mom, who has a hearing deficiency and wears hearing aids, did not find this to be as lovely as those of us who were making the music together. She came up the steps into the room we were in and shrieked, "Will you guys just stop!" When she screeched the word "stop," my biggest bowl shattered into several pieces. I was mortified! It was my favorite bowl. And it was expensive!

The energy she put forth was so strong that it caused my bowl to shatter. It was the intent behind the statement for us to stop that caused that shatter. I didn't know for years afterwards, but she knew she had broken that bowl, even though she wasn't anywhere close to it. That story depicts to me, and hopefully to you, that we don't have to be touching anything to have an impact on it with our intent and with the emotions that we have behind our words. So I invite you to be very intentional about how you throw your words around because they affect, not just you, but things and people in your environment in ways you may or may not know.

Steps and Methods

There is an intention behind some statements that seem neutral, and yet produce a negative outcome. Here are some steps to avoid the pitfalls of negative intentions:

Go deep within to determine your actual intent behind things you say. For example, if you compliment someone on what they are wearing, and deep within you are jealous that they can afford nice things and you can't, the compliment will not be received well and the words will have a negative effect. There are several ways that nice people can really have negative intentions (you can check yourself, and watch for this in others):

- Do you repeatedly ask people to do things for you with an

underlying assumption that they can help you satisfy your agenda?

- Do you sap people's energy due to negative or demanding desires?

- Is your eye contact and body language authentic, or contrived? People who can't make eye contact are uncomfortable to be around.

- Do you use persuasion or peer pressure to get what you want or to have people do what you don't want to do? Be careful not to use manipulation tactics in your favor.

- Are humor and insults how you compliment, followed with "just kidding?" This is a backhanded compliment that usually has a painful need behind it.

- Do you dominate a conversation, and always turn it toward something about you? Are you an overt attention seeker? Though this may be a more difficult one to realize, pay attention to it.

These traits are always easier to notice in someone else; however, we are better served to watch for them in ourselves while being cautious to not be pulled down by them from others.

Be vigilant with your own inner work so you will always mean what you say, without an underlying intention. Our overall frequency includes the level that we brought with us when we came into this world, plus the accumulation of storage from the emotional trauma we have experienced throughout our lives. This storage can affect the words that we think and say. The more we do our inner work to clear out the emotional storage within us, the higher the frequency of our thoughts and intentions will be.

Feel into the emotions of your words to discover your intention. There are times when I will offer an opinion about something without the idea that there may be emotion behind it, yet it comes out forceful and defensive. When that happens, I try to notice it and later reflect on what was really behind that opinion. Why was it laced with angry energy? Why is that belief something I needed to defend with such intensity? There is usually a hidden story waiting to be unearthed, recognized, and worked through.

Wisely choose your use of idioms. For example, many people use the saying, "Killing two birds with one stone," or accomplishing two things with one effort. But the idea itself is very low frequency because it refers to killing, and therefore it will produce a negative effect, even if you don't mean it to. Could we replace it with something like, "That was a twin win?" Here are other idioms with difficult energy and a higher energy option:

"To beat a dead horse" means to continue talking about something that is already over. Upgrade to, "That's water under the bridge."

"To go down in flames" means to fail miserably at something. Upgrade to, "Just gained one more lesson!"

"To kill time" means to do something for the sake of passing the time while you're waiting for another thing to occur. Upgrade to, "Waiting patiently."

"Curiosity killed the cat" means being inquisitive may get you into trouble. Upgrade to, "Curiosity sparks creativity."

The intention behind our thoughts and words is the afterburner sending that energy out into the world. Its impact can produce a positive or negative effect, depending on the intention. My goal is that you realize and schedule the time you need to uncover the hidden energy within you that charges the intention behind your words. This crucial work will reform the energy you send out and heighten the experiences in your life.

Your experiences matter. Share them with us so we can support you in your journey, or visit us here.

SCAN ME

Words Can Heal Your Life

We are all healers. Each of us has the power to heal ourselves. In fact, no one is better equipped to heal ourselves than we are.

Each of our thoughts and words provides either a healing effect or a negative effect on our bodies.

Here we will explore the truth of this. I will share stories from two books about how this is done, and will provide the following methods for you to use to achieve this yourself:

- Listen to your body.

- Hear the messages your body is telling you.

- Use manifestation techniques.

We are programmed to believe that healing is achieved only through medical professionals and that our medical destiny is in the hands of others. It is my hope that the following information will ignite a spark of belief in your own healing powers and that you will then practice until your belief becomes a reality.

In Masuro Emoto's book, Hidden Messages in Water, he shares research where he took beakers of water and set words next to them. He chose words that were high frequency, such as love and gratitude, and low-frequency, such as evil and the statement, "You disgust me." He then had people walk by those beakers and read the words in their minds. The next step was to freeze the beakers of water. Inside the freezer, he took slivers of this water and examined them under a microscope. He found that words of love and gratitude showed up in the water molecules as beautiful snowflakes with beautiful Mandala-like designs. Quite the opposite occurred with the words of low-frequency evil and disgust. There was not any kind of pattern in the water, but something you might find in the bottom of a dirty toilet.

If our bodies are 70% to 80% water, and we're using these low-frequency words on a regular basis, what is happening to our cells? What is happening to the water that is in our body? If we continue using low-frequency thoughts and words, our bodies have to be affected in a negative way.

In Louise Hay's book, You Can Heal Your Life, she lists possible ailments, followed by the potential message behind the ailment, and then affirmations that can shift frequency in our body from the ailment energy to healthy energy. I have often referred to this book with my clients. The messages are written in the form of affirmations that you can repeat to yourself for whatever ailment you might have — they can provide a healing impact on whatever ails you. Your thoughts and your intentions raise the frequency of the words that you speak, that you think, and that you listen to, and with them you can raise the frequency of your life.

Steps and Methods

If we have aches and pains, or even chronic illness, it is possible, and even plausible, that we can heal that malady using just thoughts and words. Here's how:

Our body is an intricate messaging system with the mission to support you fully. Each part of our body sends us subtle messages. If our hands are hurting, we might be holding on to life with too tight of a grip. Or if our hip is hurting, we may be hesitating to move forward in life with ease. Or if our knee is hurting, we may have an issue with being inflexible in life. Each body area provides a unique message that can be similar to someone else experiencing a similar ailment, but may also have subtle differences because each of us is unique in our experiences of life.

How you can start the healing process. Take inventory of your body's pain and see what the subtle message may be. Sit in meditation and ask your body if there is more to know.

- Find a quiet place where you will not be disturbed or distracted.

- Sit quietly with your spine straight sitting forward on the chair so your back is not supported.

- Close your eyes and relax your body and mind, in preparation for a connection experience.

- Say a prayer, inviting the deity of your choice to be with you during this experience.

- Take three deep, gentle breaths to calm your body and your mind.

- Use four successive exhalations to go deeper into your consciousness.

- Take a deep breath in, and on the exhale, say in your mind, 'I release my conscious mind' — and feel it happening.

- Take another deep breath, and on the exhalation say in your mind, "I release the unconscious mind" — and feel it happen.

- Take another deep breath, and on the exhalation, say to yourself, 'I release the subconscious mind' — and feel another layer release.

- Take another deep breath and exhale, saying to yourself, 'I release any other layer that is not my highest God self.'

- On the next inhalation, breathe in the fullest expression of your highest God-self.

- Ask your highest God-self what you need to know to heal your ailment. And listen. The answers will come in as pictures, or thoughts or words. Believe what messages say, and create an action plan for following it.

Healing your body is similar to manifestation. The most effective manifestation happens when you have a desire, and then you act as though you already have it, using all your senses. If you have a pain in your hip that has been bothering you for awhile, and you want that hip pain to go away, and you have received the message that your hip pain is telling you (this is key for healing it permanently), start your manifestation process.

- Feel with deep feeling how happy you are with your hip working perfectly, and your life moving forward into new, exciting projects.

- See yourself walking with comfort and ease. Every experience has to be what you want, not what you don't want. For example, you don't want to see yourself walking without pain; you want to see yourself walking with comfort and ease.

- Experience other areas of your life that you are successfully participating in, because your hip is whole and healthy.

- This one is the key — deeply experience a state of gratitude and joy because you are a healthy, whole, and perfect person who can do anything you want to do. In manifesting, saying it is not enough. You must also feeeeeeel it into being.

- Watch and celebrate as your body responds favorably to the shift in your energy and heals the very area you were focusing on.

- Express gratitude to your body part for its positive response to your efforts, and its ongoing effort to assist you in your life journey in a grace-filled way.

I encourage you to be an active participant in your own healing.

Chapter 9

How Our Thoughts Affect Our Emotional Health

Have you ever experienced a painful event, such as being fired, injured, or possibly a loss of relationship? This is when our thoughts can become our worst enemies. They can loop out of control and cause drastic damage to our sense of self, which often leads to depression, anxiety, mood disorders, and other mental, emotional, and even physical ailments.

Here we will explore how this happens. I will share my own story of deep depression and how I recovered using these techniques:

- Realize the thought is just passing through.

- The only hold they have on you is the one you give them.

- Hear, but don't identify with them.

- Clear your inner turmoil.

Depression causes people to be completely locked inside their own prison. There are ways out, and my hope is you will use this information to gain control of your thoughts so you can fully experience the beauty of life.

I worked at a collegiate institution for 28 years. After a miscommunication, I was relieved of duties, rather abruptly. I had known for a few years that I needed to move on, but being let go so suddenly took its toll on me emotionally. Before this, I hadn't even believed in or given much thought to depression or anxiety. But I spiraled into a depressive state due to the painful dialogue in my head and the feeling of being so harshly rejected.

The dialogue and rejection were telling me that I was let go because I wasn't valuable, that I was somehow flawed, that no one liked me at my institution. This feeling was compounded because none of my work friends or colleagues reached out to me afterwards. I felt that I was not valuable to anyone. It was time for me to move into another chapter of my life.

But my heart was hurt. As a result of that pain, I had created a story around the circumstances. That story then showed up as inner dialogue that I wasn't paying attention to because I was so hurt and immersed in my own pain. Because of my gifts of vision, I started seeing a Pigpen-type of cloud around me (you remember Pigpen from the Charlie Brown comics, who always had a cloud of dust around him). I could actually see this dark cloud and I knew that I was hurting, but I didn't know how much I was hurting. And the dialogue kept playing, though this dialog didn't have much, if any truth to it, yet because it was nonstop, I believed it.

That is the way with anything, if you hear it enough times, you believe it. None of it was true, and the truth was that it was time for me to move to the next chapter of my life.

Be mindful of your thoughts, especially after you have had a traumatic situation.

Hold in your tool box the truth that the universe is never working against you, that it is always working for you.

Steps and Methods

When you control your thoughts, it drastically improves your mental health. It is that easy, and yet a seemingly daunting task. We can knock down the villains in our heads through the following techniques:

Realize the inner dialogue is just passing thoughts. All thoughts are like leaves blowing in the wind. Trouble comes when we latch onto those passing thoughts as truths about ourselves. I refer to our ego as the human aspect of our existence. The ego is the hurt aspect of you reacting to pain and drama and the perceptions it has created about who you are based on those traumas and dramas.

Passing thoughts only have power over you if you allow it. We tend to believe the ongoing inner dialog because it plays nonstop 24/7. Even someone like me, who's done positive affirmations for years, can hold back the dialogue only for the time you're focused on the affirmations. Then the Inner Gremlin begins again. If we can change our perception and beliefs about those thoughts, that is the first step in overcoming the impact they can have on us.

Though you can hear them, do not identify with them. In other words, don't take them personally. Yes, they are repetitive; yes, they can be painful; yes, they seem true, and when you can take the sting out of them by giving them a lower status, that is a good start. What does that mean?

If a small random child called you a name, would you take it personally? Most reasonable adults would chuckle at the idea of a little person making such a claim, but would not believe it was true. The dialogue loop is merely the perspective of your hurt inner child. It is NOT about YOU, the adult. When we finally listen to the needs of that little one without judgment, and with compassion, the healing begins.

Do your inner shadow work to clear out the inner turmoil. As the layers of stored emotions from the traumas of the past are released, the dialog will diminish and eventually stop. This is the most valuable work you get to do for yourself as an awakened soul. Elevation of consciousness will not happen until we are able to unearth the emotions held within and unveil the being of light that you truly are.

There are many ways you can do this. My recommendation is to connect with a shadow work healer who can assist you. I did it myself, and it took 16 years. The value of this is that I now have a technique from Source that gets to the core of the stored emotions quickly, brings them to the surface to be healed, and then we heal them. There are others doing similar work. Gift yourself this sacred experience from me or others. It can be done at a distance or in person.

Spiraling negative thoughts will never have a positive effect on you and your health. And there are ways to overcome them. My hope is that you will take this information seriously and apply it to your life. Gaining control of your thoughts, even eventually erasing them, and you will instantly experience a life of emotional and personal freedom.

Start today.

The Potential of Thoughts — The Truth of Manifestation

Our lives are a demonstration of the thoughts we think. All

thoughts we think are actually prayers or manifestations of "requests." Do you like what you have in your life? If not, it is time to change your process.

Here we will explore the path to manifestation. I will tell you a cute story of the fastest manifestation I can remember happening for me, and we will discuss the following steps to help you to start manifesting what you do want today:

- Focus on what you do want, not what you don't want.

- Add emotion, which is energy in motion.

- Stay away from the energy of wanting.

- Whatever you already have, you can reach for the next level.

- Live as if your dream is already yours.

- Watch for the full desire to materialize,

One hot day I was standing out in my yard. The temperature was in the 90s, and I needed to mow the lawn. But it was so hot that I didn't want to start. I ruminated on possible solutions, wondering if I should hire one of those lawn companies to come and quickly mow the lawn for me. I went inside and shifted my thinking to something else.

Within the hour, there was a knock at the door. A teenager stood there. He told me he lived down the street and was looking for a way to make money. He asked, "Would you like me to mow your lawn?"

I burst out laughing, not because I didn't appreciate the concept, but because it was a manifestation that came so quickly!

I said, "YES, I would! Do you want to use my mower or yours?" So that was my experience of a manifestation that happened in less than an hour — and it demonstrates the power of our thoughts.

Steps and Methods

If you want abundance in your life, you must think abundantly. If you want a Tesla, you must act as if you already have a Tesla to drive. You get what you resonate with. It's that easy. And of course, if we are steeped in the middle of difficult feelings, it doesn't seem that easy to make the leap from depression to bliss. In fact, you don't even have to. What is the path to get what you want?

Focus on what you do want, not what you don't want. We all get to manifest literally with every thought that we think. So why not manifest exactly what we do want, instead of trying to avoid what we don't want? The Universe does not understand words of lack. So we always want to focus on what we do want. And when we focus on what we do want, and we put emotion behind it, and then what we do want comes to fruition.

What kind of emotion am I referring to? We want to feel as though we already have it. We want to resonate with the frequency of already owning it. For example, if you would like to have a car, what kind of car do you want? Make up your mind and step into the consciousness of knowing it's possible. If you carry out the attitude that you are already an owner of that kind of car, the car will show up. It has to. It's the way the universe works. It's the way Source works. The truth is that we are always manifesting based on our thoughts and our emotions. Look at what surrounds you — this is manifestation. If you don't like what you see, you must change your thoughts. I encourage you to manifest exactly what you do want and take your focus off what you don't want.

Stay out of the energy of wanting. As a matter of curiosity, you can identify what you are already manifesting by evaluating what you already have in your life. Do you like what you have? If so, you are already on the right path. If you would like something different, set your desires without being in the energy of wanting.

What's next? What do you already have? Use this information to determine the next step up in your life. It is possible to make a leap from anger to bliss, but it is not likely. When we feel bad, people who are blissful nauseate us. Their unbridled happiness does not seem real and therefore not even desired. So, it is wise to just seek the next better feeling or thought or elevation in your desires — instead of reaching for bliss, reach from anger to courage.

Act as if you are already living that next transformational step. If you live in anger, practice experiencing courage. Just decide to be courageous, actually fully commit to it, and it will happen. Or, instead of just wanting a Lexus or Acura, embody the feeling that you are a Lexus or an Acura owner.

And then wait for the full expression of your desires to materialize in your life.

Our Thoughts and Our Health

Your thoughts can take you to wonderful places and to strange places. Your thoughts can make you elated or can make you miserable. Your thoughts have a tremendous effect on your health.

We can't feel good about ourselves if we're thinking we're inadequate. If we feel bad, it is because we are having bad thoughts, and most of them are unconscious thoughts. For most of my life, my mind was feeding me endless negative information about me, my place in life, my ability for success, how I looked, my athletic prowess, and so much more. As a result of this all-day and all-night negative feeding of my mind, I was filled with self-doubt, self-loathing, insecurities about myself and how I fit in the world, and I had diminished ability for success in my work and my relationships, both with myself and others. And I was sure everyone had this crazy thinking going on, that it was just a fact of life. But this is not the case. It wasn't the case for me, and it isn't the case for you.

Uncontrolled negative thinking is a habit that has become an addiction. There is a solution, and that solution is right here for you.

As far as I can remember, I had a negative dialogue going on in my head, which had a negative effect on my mental and physical health. I didn't realize any of it because I wasn't paying attention to the dialogue. It was just playing thoughts in my head, nonstop, behind the scenes.

One day when I was running on the track, I became aware of these thoughts, which were of proving to someone who wasn't there that what I had done was the right thing. And I presented the "proof" from a variety of different angles or circumstances. Once I noticed this dialogue, I began to pay attention to it. Eventually, I realized my brain was talking to me all the time, and it was essentially criticizing me all the time.

I now ask my clients about it, and everyone has some sort of dialogue going on. Most people can even recite some of what they hear. I now call this inner dialogue my Inner Gremlin. This Inner Gremlin is not telling the truth. The things being said are not true. They are made up. What do we need to do to extinguish our Inner Gremlin?

How can we feel good about ourselves if a recording plays on a loop in our mind about our inadequacies? We can't. I am living proof. If we feel bad, it is because we are having bad thoughts, and most of them are unconscious thoughts. For most of my life, my mind was feeding me endless negative information about myself, my place in life, my ability for success, how I looked, my athletic prowess, and so much more. As a result of this 24/7/365 negativity, I was filled with self-doubt, self-loathing, and insecurities about myself. I had diminished ability for success in my work and my relationships with myself and others. I was sure that everyone had this crazy thinking, that it was just a fact of life.

That dialogue can stop. It did for me. A few years ago, I noticed the repeated negative dialogue in my head was no longer there. That subtle yet monumental experience has completely changed the way I engage with myself. Everyone can experience this kind of transformation with some simple steps. It takes persistence, but it is doable, and you absolutely want to delve into this, starting today.

Steps and Methods

Here are some steps to take.

Recognize that negative thought loops are present. They can look like talking about yourself negatively in public, or cursing at yourself for "screwing up," or like me, ongoing inner conversations defending your actions in one way or another, or other individual possibilities.

Realize the dialogue is not YOU talking to YOU. It is actually old voices of your life that were recorded in your subconscious and are playing randomly at vulnerable moments

Write a rebuttal. Even if your ego says it is true, get your journal out and write at the top of a new page the dialogue you caught your inner self chanting. Then make a list of accomplishments that demonstrate what is being said is a lie. For example, if you are hearing your inner self saying nobody likes you, on your paper write examples of all the people who do like you, and evidence of how you know that, such as, "Sally stops by weekly and brings me cookies," or "Everyone at the grocery store smiles when I walk past." Prove to yourself through your list that the negative dialogue is simply not true.

Repeat this process for every self-defeating statement you hear in your head or that comes rolling off your tongue.

My hope is you use these techniques to find your own emotional freedom. There are a few little-known studies that prove these habits can go away, and you have the tools that can make it happen.

You Can Change the Way You Think — and Your Life

The life we seek is not beyond our reach, regardless of where we begin.

Here, we will explore a formula to shift your life. I will share with you my personal experience of going from lack to luxury, and I will give you the following clues to assist you in your transformation:

- Take inventory of the way your friends communicate.

- Surround yourself with the kind of people you want to be.

- Embody the energy of a prosperous person.

My hope is that you will take to heart these techniques and use them to your highest benefit. You deserve a life that you love, and it is certainly within your reach.

The clues that I had around me for so much of my life were that all of my associates were living in a state of lack. And some of my friends were living in a state of victimhood. The majority of the people in my life were people who didn't have much money, who were unable to travel, unable to invest and to improve their life in financial ways. You may have heard that you are a representation of your five closest friends. When I looked around at my five closest friends, I realized I needed to change my friends, and not because these people weren't wonderful people I liked and ap-preciated —, but because I needed to be under the influence of people who were in the energy that I wanted to be in.

I have done much inner work to release the layers and layers and layers of low-frequency energy that were holding me back and keeping me from being able to feel that elevated life and level of consciousness. I was able to align myself with those who had high frequency energy, and who were illustrations of what I actually sought in my own life.

I invite you to be very mindful of those people in your circle. What are they showing you about YOU? It is not about judging, reject-ing, or looking down on others — it is about being the example for them to also join you in the higher vibration as you surround yourself with other high frequency friends.

Steps and Methods

We can truly transform our lives by transforming our thoughts. Use this process for ultimate success:

Take inventory of how the people in your circle communi-cate. Communication is a reflection of the way they think. Do they speak about ideas, or about people? If they are speaking about people, this is a sure sign you convene with people who are not working on improving themselves. Because we are a reflection of the five closest people in our circle, it is necessary to take inven-tory of how you are reflecting on the world. If the people in your life demonstrate low-level communication, it is likely you do, too. Speaking about ideas is the highest form of communication. Seek out people who focus on their own personal growth and have a mission of serving others.

Surround yourself with high-quality people. Pay attention to communication patterns of the high quality people you are sur-rounding yourself with. Pay attention to what they focus on. Pay attention to their interests related to growth. Pay attention to their life mission. People who are growing and serving spend a greater percentage of their time thinking high frequency thoughts. Be-cause energy and thoughts are transferable through the ethers, you will be absorbing high energy thoughts from them that will influence the way you think, as well.

Embody Prosperity Consciousness: Embody the energy of a prosperous person. Prosperity is not just about money. Prosperity Consciousness is a state of being, not just a state of doing. Most people misidentify and misapply that prosperity consciousness is something that they can only find outside of themselves. In truth, it is a state of being that comes from within.

Be around the energy of the people who have what you desire, and BE the energy of the thing you want, and the Universe has to bring it to you. It is your CHOICE! You can choose to keep on creating your life based on limitations, or you can decide you are prosperous and your life and your experiences will reflect exactly that.

Are you ready for a new beginning? Embody these procedures and use them for your greatest personal gain. You deserve to live in a way that exemplifies your dreams.

Let's get started today.

Chapter 10

How to Cope with Trauma and Toxicity

Throughout our lives, we navigate experiences that cause deep, long lasting, emotional pain. When the pain is too great, we don't have the tools ourselves to be able to properly "dispose" of it, so it is stored in our bodies. This causes blockages in our energy flow and, ultimately, emotional issues and illness as we age. And most of the time the parents or adult figures in our lives are not self-realized enough to be able to assist us, either.

I learned a great deal about the impact of childhood experiences on adult behaviors. I've learned enormously about the layers of emotional trauma that we each store within us.

Are you ready to face the trauma and the challenges of your past? When the pain is too great, we don't have the tools ourselves to be able to properly "dispose" of it, so it is stored in our bodies, causing blockages in our energy flow and ultimately emotional issues and physical illness as we age.

Here is how we can change that:

- Identify your core shadow belief.

- Identify the area in your body where that emotional belief is stored.

- Identify the actual emotions that are stored.

- Identify the age you were when you stored them.

- Nurture the "little you" in the way you needed it at the time of the trauma.

It is our job to take the necessary steps to work through the traumas so our lives can resonate at the frequency of peace.

I've spent many years uncovering and unpeeling all of the density that I've had stored within. I have always been energetically sensitive. When there was turmoil in the household as a child, I would find my way outside to be in a place of peace. I spent my earliest years on a farm with my immediate family, surrounded by aunts and uncles, cousins, and both sets of grandparents; everything that I knew of as love was on or near our farm. To me this was bliss. When my parents divorced and Mom took my sisters and me to live three hours away, my foundation was obliterated. My sense of safety and love exploded, leaving inner pain and trauma buried within.

I had no idea this enormous life shift had such an impact. Within a year, Mom remarried, and our stepfather introduced us to the Unity Church. I began attending and learning their principles of the power of positive thinking and that God is love. I was immediately exposed to a tremendous amount of positivity after the devastatingly traumatic life shift. It would seem with this exposure long-term effects would be minimal.

The Unity church was continuously a part of my life until I was out of college. I immersed myself in this positive influence and abundant love each Sunday, as well as summer camp each summer. After college, I added to my self-development through Dale Carnegie classes, which is about being aware of the thoughts of your mind and taking control of your life. We studied books such as, How to Win Friends and Influence People, and How to Stop Worrying and Start Living, among others. Throughout my entire life, I read mainly positive spiritual material. Guidepost magazine, which was about positive thinking, was always on my nightstand. Norman Vincent Peale was the author of that magazine, and he was a major influencer in the philosophy of positive thinking. This exposure to personal development was in my life constantly.

Sometime when I was in my late 40s, I realized, even after all of this training, that I still had an enormous sense of self-doubt. After substantial contemplation and realizing all the study I had been involved in, this just didn't make any sense. I need to really look into it.

At the time I was reading Divine Revelation, a book by Susan Shumsky in which she describes a technique for receiving divine answers to questions very quickly, every time you ask. I haven't read the book in a long time, so I might have created my own technique based on her influence, but the basic concept is there.

I dove into finding the answers with great intensity, because I was going to get to the bottom of this impending sense of self-doubt. Shumsky's process is about releasing all levels of consciousness until you get to your highest God consciousness, and then asking your desired question.

My question was, "What is with this impending sense of self-doubt?" And in my mind's eye I saw an image of my father leaving. He was sitting in his car, and my sisters and I were standing next to the car. I had a bird's eye perspective. Interestingly, I have seen this same picture over and over again throughout my life. I just kept thinking it was a memory. It would pop up in my mind and I would think, 'Oh, there's that memory again.' This time I had the wherewithal to say telepathically, 'I've seen that picture before — what does it mean?' And the next thought that came to my mind was, 'If your father would leave you, it means he doesn't love you, and if he doesn't love you, no one will.'

I'd been holding onto that shadow belief for all those years. Was it responsible for my ongoing sense of self-doubt? It made sense that if I didn't feel loved or lovable, I'd make decisions that were different than if I had felt loved and lovable.

That was the beginning of learning about the layers of emotional trauma I had stored within me. Since then, I have uncovered multiple layers of trauma emotions that have been stored within me that I didn't know were there, for instance, emotional trauma of abandonment from getting my tonsils removed when I was five and had to stay in the hospital overnight. Parents weren't allowed to stay all night at the hospital in those days. It was scary to be there alone at age five. I had had trauma from losing my blanket when I was four, actually blaming myself for the devastating loss, and there was trauma from lost love experiences as I went through my teens and twenties.

Over the past 16 years, I've uncovered many layers of emotional trauma that were altering the truth of who I am and preventing my energy centers from being fully open.

It is vital for you to do your own inner work so you can raise your frequency, your consciousness, and your perspective on life, as well as the frequency of the planet. We are all here to ascend, and this is the only way to make it happen.

Steps and Methods

I was able to release these deeply seeded experiences through these steps:

Identify the core shadow that comes from painful trauma. The core shadow belief or beliefs are the perceptions of yourself of who you are as a result of pain. Our original, unhurt self resonates from a pure angel-like perspective without any hurts that taint our belief of who we are. Core shadow beliefs put a stamp on us that makes us feel 'less than" in some way. Some typical Core Shadow Beliefs are:

- Something is wrong with me.

- I cannot trust anyone.

- I'm a bad person.

- I'm not lovable.

- I don't deserve to have what I want.

- Love does not last.

- I am worthless.

- I am never going to be successful.

Identify where in your body that energy was stored. We can quiet our thoughts and pay attention to where we feel tightness, or discomfort. Sometimes we already have an ailment that is a clue to where we might be storing emotions. To take a body inventory, I like to use the body inventory meditation:

- Sit in a comfortable position, feet on the floor, your hands on your lap, facing up to receive or facing down to feel grounded. Be certain your spine is straight.

- Take three deep, gentle breaths in through your nose and out through your mouth. With each exhale, allow your body to relax even more.

- Imagine your focus is a scanner that slowly focuses on individual areas of your body to see where there is tightness or discomfort. Pay attention to subtle indications of tenseness and also those that are strong.

  - Start at the top of your head and scan your whole head.

  - Then scan your neck, shoulders, arms, and hands.

  - Then scan your entire upper torso, front and back, and around your lungs and heart.

  - Move down to your lower torso. Feel into the intestines and the reproductive areas.

  - Move down to your hips and thighs, and then your knees, low legs, and feet.

Where was the tightness? Where was the discomfort? Journal all the areas you found that were experiencing tightness or discomfort. You want to address the most uncomfortable ones first.

Now that you know the location or locations, identify the emotions that are stored. Reflecting on your most-used emotion when you are triggered, or settle into a calm state and see what emotions come forward when you say your Shadow Belief in your mind. If you say, "I'm not lovable," how does that make you feel?

Identify the age that you stored those emotions. This can be an easy process just by asking for your inner child to "show up" and ask yourself, "How old are you?" Or you can use the clues. How old do you behave when you are triggered? A few weeks ago when I got triggered, I went to my bedroom, curled into a ball, and cried. While it is okay to cry, this behavior demonstrated a much younger me. Fetal position represents a very young little one.

Releasing the emotion is the next step. You can do this just as I did, by nurturing the little you that experienced that particular trauma and was never supported or loved in the manner necessary to prevent storing that inner pain. You can say the things that "little you" needed to hear, and provide the kind of loving support that little you needed to experience.

This is what I do:

- "See" the little you in your mind's eye wherever he or she is, or just pretend they are there.

- Approach them gently. Often, they do not trust adults; after all, adults are the ones who disappointed them.

- Develop rapport with them by sending a wave of love from your adult heart to their little heart. Love is the most powerful healer, so keep it flowing into their heart.

- Begin saying what they (you) always needed to hear. All this can be mentally or out loud. They are very good at hearing either way.

When you follow this process, long-stored emotions will be burned off and dissipate into the atmosphere, and that emotional trigger will no longer be present. This is called "doing your inner work." This is the truth that sets you free.

Your Body's Physical Toxicity

Everyone's body holds toxicity. These toxins are responsible for all health conditions we may be experiencing.

Here, we explore solutions to this worldwide problem. I will share my own story of releasing toxins and the shocking surprise that resulted. I will give you the process I used:

- Use the proven ancient techniques of Siddha Veda.

- Eat mung bean soup.

- Add specific herbs for your circumstances.

- Fill the energetic void with high frequency energy.

- Add positive affirmations to your day.

My 88-years-young father was experiencing cognitive decline that resulted in him failing his driver's exam. I temporarily moved in with him and guided him through this exact process. It cleared up his mind, and he is now a licensed driver and continues to live independently.

My hope for you is for relief from whatever you are struggling with. There are support Zoom calls every Sunday on AncientSecretsZoom.com with people from all over the world, and everyone is cordially invited to join for support in your healing.

I had a bewildering yet powerful experience with the Siddha Veda detox program that comes through the Ayushakti Clinic in Mumbai, India. This clinic has a program where you pay $20 to speak with a doctor of Siddha Veda medicine.

They use ancient Indian science to evaluate you via Zoom, and provide you with more information from their assessment than I have ever received through an allopathic medical appointment. Ayushakti often recommends a detoxification program, and that was the case with me, as well.

My first experience with an Ayushakti detoxification program was symbolic because it cleansed and purified density out of me in ways that were new and surprising. I had already gone through three other detox programs over the course of the previous four years. I feel I had a pretty good handle on what was going on with body detoxification.

I've mentioned how the pandemic years led many of us, including me, to be less active and eat less healthily. I didn't even grow my normal vegetables. Access to fresh food was diminished due to a reduction in shopping and having no local farmers' markets in operation.

The program entails a regime of mung bean soup made in a special way, and bottles of herbs recommended by the Ayushakti clinic. My mission was to follow the guidelines precisely. In my opinion if you're going to make a commitment, it's easier to do it 100% than to give yourself a pass every once in a while.

Day one begins with fasting and drinking the tea with the prescribed herbs. Day 2 and beyond was a schedule of mung bean soup and herbs, to go along with some tea, and water intake. This program was quite astounding because, in five days I had eliminated six pounds of stored waste from my body. Throughout the whole process, my elimination improved dramatically, and it was pretty good already.

This detox was unloading toxins that had been stored in my body for an unknown period of time. Elimination was like clockwork, first thing when I woke up each the morning.

According to Siddha Veda, morning elimination is vitally important, yet it is not emphasized in the western ways, and therefore most of us don't do it. This detox wanted to teach my body what was supposed to happen, and it worked. This was the first time I'd had that kind of schedule. I've got to say it felt really fabulous, physically.

What I was also finding is that it felt fabulous emotionally, too. As we clear out our intestines, including the liver and gallbladder, it is likely we would clear out emotions. Along with doing their other job of filtering toxins, our liver and gallbladder store emotions, especially anger. If we have that inside of us, and we start cleansing and purifying the toxins from the food and waste, the toxic load from the emotions begin to unfurl, as well. This is what happened to me, and I didn't even realize I had stored anger.

During a five-day online meditation retreat, the fury came bubbling forth. You wouldn't think that during a meditation retreat, anger would be coming up, but it did. And it came up with a fury. I was shocked at how angry I became. Of course, social graces would make sure that I would be holding my tongue and not spreading this anger all around.

But each day at the end of our retreat, when the cameras were off, I erupted, to no one, about no one. It was strange. I couldn't figure out what it was about — it was just anger spewing out. And I was out of control. I had never experienced myself like that, and I knew it was important to allow these emotions that had been stuck inside me for so long to unfurl, and to let that energy burn off.

These emotions took me by complete surprise. There was repeated yelling. It was intense, and there was also heavy crying and even screaming. There was no one in the house that this was directed at. My animals were the only ones home, and they were innocent bystanders. I have never been a yeller, or a screamer.

This was highly unusual behavior for me. I looked like a crazy person and wondered where this could be coming from. At some point God became my target. I told her all about how angry I was and demanded to know what it was all about. Since this is no way to get answers, there were none delivered, but the emotions were expended, and it was a highly traumatic experience.

At the end of this intense emotional dumping, which lasted two and half days, I was a brand-new person. Spending so much time on inner work during the meditation retreat combined with the detoxification program was the catalyst for the deepest emotional cleansing I had ever experienced. It was a long-needed inner purging.

Steps and Methods

Here is the process I went through to create my breakthrough:

Begin by using the ancient wisdom of Siddha Veda science to increase the detoxifying foods in your diet. If your health is stable and relatively good, it is likely safe for you to use the basic technique. If you have health challenges, contact Ayushakti first before initiating your detoxification process. If you should want to have an appointment with an Ayushakti Doctor to assess your health and support you through your Mung Bean Soup Detox, call (1-800) 280-0906.

The basic technique is really quite simple. Ask yourself, "Is this mung bean soup?" If it isn't, then don't eat it, with the exception of water and tea. I ate mung bean soup for every meal.

My process was assisted by reading the book, Ancient Secrets of a Master Healer: *A Western Skeptic, An Eastern Master, And Life's Greatest Secrets* (2020) by Dr. Client Rogers. That book is where I learned about this detoxification process (I provided the recipe for Mung Bean Soup earlier in this book.)

Fill the energetic gap left by releasing all that waste. Releasing so much in the way of physical and emotional waste leaves a vacuum within that will eventually be filled with something. Whenever there is anything cleared from our system, it is wise to replace it with something high frequency to fill in the gaps. What is the best way to do this?

The best way is seeing Divine light pouring in through the top of your head, allowing it to flow down through your body all the way to your feet, filling all the empty spaces, and seeing your body enveloped in light for a couple minutes or more, before moving into your day, according to Quan Yin, in Kaia Ra's Book, The Sophia Code (2016).

It is also wise to add positive affirmations to your routine to assist in reprogramming your thoughts from those of the painful emotions to those of the new, elevated emotions. Here are the basics:

Make Your Positive Affirmations Actually Positive. Use positive words. Avoid "don't" words. The Universe only understands what you are actually focusing on and what you believe is already there. Also, words with obvious negative connotations should be avoided, words like pain, anger, and disease — you are adding energy to those concepts.

So if you say, "No more back pain," you are focusing on your back and the pain, so you get more back pain. A better option is, "I have a strong and healthy back!" I love overarching concepts like, "My entire body is getting more and more healthy."

Use Present Tense for Continuous Improvement. Affirmations work only when you believe they can, and only when they are stated in a way that it is happening NOW. When you use the word "want" in any statement, it puts your desire out into the future, like you are reaching for it. And when wanting is a part of the message, the Universe responds by giving you what you want, which is to want.

So instead of saying, "I want a new land rover," say, "I am a land rover owner." If you can believe in the possibility, then the affirmation will work for you. Whenever you resist believing in your statements, consider changing the wording of your affirmations. If "I am healthy" feels wrong at the moment, say something like, "I am healing more and more every day."

Write believable and realistic statements that apply to your life circumstances. Repeat your affirmations a few times every day in a quiet place, and try to be calm and focused when you do it.

Here are some examples of powerful affirmations to propel you into your most amazing health. There are many available on the Internet. Be certain you use the guidelines to determine if they are written well and are right for you. If any are difficult for you to believe, consider adding "I am getting more and more...." to the current example.

- Perfect health is my Divine right, and I claim it now.

- I am healthy, happy, safe and secure.

- I am beautiful, strong, and powerful.

- My body is vibrant and healthy.

- I believe in myself with every fiber of my being

- I am becoming healthier every day.

- My inner beauty radiates outwards.

- I am healthy, wealthy, whole, and strong.

- I feel positive in every cell of my body.

My hope is, even if you have tried everything else and are exhausted from all the options you have attempted, that you will give this a try. People from all over the world are gaining back their movement, their cognitive abilities, their lives.

See you on the Zoom calls every Sunday at 8 am Pacific, 11 am Eastern time, here.

Emotional Pain Bodies

We all have stored childhood trauma held within our tissues that manipulate our thoughts and dictate the direction of all aspects of our lives. Healing this trauma that is held as emotional pain is vital to our lives, and it is the most valuable process we can do for ourselves. The difficult part in starting the healing process is knowing what there is to heal.

Here, we will explore the path to healing. I will share the stories of

Buddha and Jesus to demonstrate the importance of this process, and I will describe in detail the following 3-step process to uncover what you hold within so you can expedite your healing journey:

- Do a body inventory.
- Sit in meditation with the intention to reveal stored emotion.
- Use a special technique to discover layers of trauma.

If you study Buddhism or even know the story of Siddhartha Gautama, who became Buddha, you know that he grew up in a family that completely sheltered him from the trials of existence outside of his noble life. One day he escaped outside of the castle walls, from the protection of his family, to see the strife that was going on outside of those walls. It hurt him deeply to see the pain and anguish being suffered by the common people, so he made it his mission to serve them. He vowed to do everything he could to reduce strife in the world.

One of the major events of his life was when he sat under the Bodhi tree. The story says that he sat there for 49 days, with the intention of purging the dramas and traumas that he held within that were a part of his DNA, that were a part of his history, that were a part of the strife of the world outside his protected walls. It was 49 days spent releasing all this trauma from inside him. Siddhartha Gautama had to go through this release in order to achieve enlightenment and become the Buddha.

After his enlightenment, he was bestowed the title of Buddha, which means "awakened one." He could become awakened only after the release of all the traumas, which elevated the frequency of his body and allowed the body to be able to hold the highest frequency of enlightenment.

A similar story exists in the Christian religion, where we know that Jesus went into the desert for 40 days and 40 nights. What was he doing there? Of course, it was the same thing that Buddha was doing under the Bodhi tree, that is, releasing the inner traumas he was carrying from his life circumstances up to that point, as well as energetic traumas from the world at large.

Both Buddha and Jesus had to release emotional traumas that were held within them as emotional density so that they could elevate their own frequency to the highest point.

This is so imperative in our own lives. In fact, it is the single most important work we have to do on this earth. We cannot fully live our greatest life without releasing and doing our own inner work.

I invite you to employ these techniques that we are providing here so that you can experience your highest frequency and become your own saintly self.

As we discussed before, with every traumatic experience you had as a child and even later, energy is stored in your body in the form of emotions. You may have many layers of emotions stored within your tissues. With each passing year, and additional trauma events, if you haven't learned the skills to avoid the storage, you are adding to the toxic landfill of emotions within you.

Steps and Methods

Over the last 16 years of my life, I have been doing my own inner work. It took me that long because I didn't know what I was doing. Self-experimentation was my way. And now, I have learned there is a much easier and quicker way — utilizing the simple techniques outlined below. Here we assist you in finding the layers of traumas that must be resolved.

Do a body inventory feeling into your body for dense or painful areas.

- Find a quiet place where you will not be disturbed or distracted.

- Sit quietly with your spine straight sitting forward on the chair, so your back is not supported.

- Close your eyes and relax your body and mind in preparation for a connection experience.

- Say a prayer inviting the deity of your choice to be with you during this experience.

- Take 3 deep, gentle breaths to calm your body and your

mind.

- Begin a scan starting at the top of your head and slowly move down through every aspect of your body. Where do you feel tightness, soreness, a different sensation that doesn't feel "right." Make note of these in your memory.

- Return to each tight or uncomfortable location individually. Focus on that location. What does it want to tell you? When you have received the message, the discomfort can resolve.

- If you don't complete your focus on each location, be certain to return to them as soon as possible. Your higher self knows you have checked in, and will be waiting for you to complete the process.

Sit in contemplation or meditation with the intention of finding more and more stored experiences. Sometimes, our inner child is so ready to reveal their pain they just have to be called on, and they come forward providing valuable information that can lead to important breakthroughs:

Use Susan Schumsky's technique from her book, Divine Revelations, to discover the layers held within. Then continue with the bullet points listed on page 141.

- Find a quiet place where you will not be disturbed or distracted.

- Sit quietly with your spine straight, sitting forward on the chair, so your back is not supported.

- Close your eyes, and relax your body and mind in preparation for a connection experience.

- Say a prayer, inviting the deity of your choice to be with you during this experience.

- Take three deep gentle breaths, to calm your body and your mind.

- Use four successive exhales, to go deeper into your consciousness.

- Take a deep breath in, and on the exhale, say in your mind,

'I release my conscious mind,' and feel that happening.

- Take another deep breath, and on the exhale say in your mind, 'I release the unconscious mind,' and feel it happening.

- Then take another deep breath, and on the exhale, say in your mind, 'I release the subconscious mind,' and feel another layer release.

- Take another deep breath, and on the exhale, say in your mind, 'I release any other layer that is not my highest God-self.'

- On the next inhale, breathe in the fullest expression of your highest God-self.

- Ask your highest God-self to reveal the layers held within that are ready to be healed.

- Then listen. The answers will come in as pictures, or thoughts or words. Believe what the messages say, and create an action plan for following them.

- For any densities and discomforts that show up, ask for the message they are holding within. The message is the key to releasing the density.

- For any "inner children" that show up, honor them completely. Give them the love they have been desiring for a very long time, and follow this chart to clear and release the pain they have held for so long:

Steps toward Freedom	Action for you
1. Call on the wisdom of your inner child through meditation.	Ask this inner being to reveal to you what trauma or traumas are present where healing needs to occur.
2. Experience or pretend this child is right there with you as a separate individual in the room.	Feel into their presence. Determine what they need to feel whole. Is it to be held? To be honored? To be heard? To be unconditionally loved? To be spoken to with tender respect?

3. Provide them exactly what they need and have needed for so long.	a. Earn their trust slowly. Often, they do not trust adults because adults are who caused their original pain. b. Flow a continuous wave of love from your heart to theirs. c. Communicate gently to them telepathically that you are here for them and that you will honor them in every possible way. d. Speak the words of love and compassion to them they have needed to hear. e. Ask them what they would like to know or experience, and provide that for them. f. Pay attention to them and play with them as you would an invisible friend, i.e., with tea parties, playing catch, swings, ice cream treats, night time stories — mentally, of course. g. Continue this process until you experience a sense of completion, and/or they have risen into a state of pure innocence related to that original wound. This sometimes takes a couple weeks or more. h. Repeat the process. We hold many layers and experiences of stuck emotions. With the release of each trauma, we experience more and more inner freedom

We are here to support you. If you have questions, reach out to us here.

Chapter 11

The Frequency of Music

Music is not only the food of love, but of life itself.

Though we often like music similar to what we grew up with, it is wise to learn about the music you hear and that you make a point of listening to. This is to determine whether it is affecting you in positive ways or negative ways.

Music is energy. The sounds from music travel through the air in measurable waves, or frequencies, that have an effect on us when they travel into our ears and transmit to our brains. Do you have a favorite song? When you turn it on, do you feel warm inside, want to dance and sing along, instantly improving your mood? What about a song you really hate that feels like you're listening to nails on a chalkboard, and actually puts you in an off mood? Well, blame the frequency.

I will share a story of how our music tuning was changed for covert reasons, and offer you the highest frequency music to enjoy:

- Solfeggio tones
- Gregorian Chants
- Sanskrit Chants

In 1988, biochemist Dr. Glen Rein made a discovery that confirmed what the ancient spiritual traditionalists understood when he tested the impact of different music on human DNA. Dr. Rein exposed similar DNA vials to four kinds of music with different frequencies – Gregorian chants, Sanskrit chants, classical, and rock. By measuring the rate of UV light absorption, an essential function of healthy DNA, Rein was able to assess the effects of each type of music.

The results will make you reconsider the type of music you listen to when you want to relax. The Gregorian and Sanskrit chants had the most positive, and even healing, effects by increasing UV light absorption between 5 to 9 percent.

Classical music increased UV absorption by small amounts. And rock music decreased UV light absorption, harming the DNA. Rein's research supported the theory that sound frequencies do produce serious effects, for better or worse, on health and well-being.

In addition, nature is aligned with frequencies that are connected to the numbers 3, 6, and 9. Nikola Tesla said, "If you only knew the magnificence of the 3, 6, and 9, then you would hold a key to the universe." These numbers were sacred in ancient times, as they did promise to unlock the secrets to the universe. The numbers 3, 6, and 9 are the fundamental root vibrations of the Solfeggio frequencies.

The frequency of ancient music was based on 432 Hz, which is a pure mathematical tone. Current music is based on the frequency of 440 Hz.

432 is based on the 3, 6, 9 concept through the Pythagorean reduction process used in numerology. 432 = 4+3+2= 9, but 440 breaks down in a similar way to 8, which is not a number associated with nature and is dissonant to our own body's frequency.

432 is a superior tuning that makes music easier to listen to and more enjoyable because it's consistent with patterns of the universe. At this frequency, our bodies and minds work in perfect harmony. It is interesting to know the number 432 can be seen in many ancient structures.

The 432 Hz frequency is known to release emotional blockages and expand consciousness. It assists in putting us in harmony with the frequency of the Universe. It allows us to be more connected with the innate knowledge of the Universe in a more intuitive way.

Though we tend to like similar music that we grew up with, it is wise to learn about the music you are listening to and see whether it is likely affecting you in positive ways or negative ways. There are possibilities of having neutral effects also, which are certainly better than negative effects.

Steps and Methods

The quality of music we listen to has a major part to play in our emotional and physical well-being. Even Confucius had something to say about it:

> "If one should desire to know whether a kingdom is well governed, if its morals are good or bad, the quality of its music will furnish the answer."

Solfeggio Tones. Solfeggio frequencies make up the ancient 6-tone scale thought to have been used in sacred music, including Gregorian chants. Each Solfeggio tone holds a specific frequency that balances your energy and keeps your body, mind, and spirit in perfect harmony. The original scale was six ascending notes assigned to Ut-Re-Mi-Fa-Sol-La. The six main Solfeggio frequencies are:

- 396 Hz for liberating one from fear and guilt

- 417 Hz frequencies for facilitating change and undoing situations

- 528 Hz for miracles and transformations like DNA repair

- 639 Hz frequencies for relationships and reconnecting

- 741 Hz solfeggio frequencies for getting solutions and expressing themselves

- 852 Hz frequencies for returning one to a spiritual order

Today, we know the Solfeggio scale as seven ascending notes assigned to the syllables Do-Re-Mi-Fa-So-La-Ti.

Our modern day musical scale is out of sync when compared with the original Solfeggio scale. If we want to bring harmony into our lives, we need to replace the dissonant western scale of 440 Hz with nature's harmony in the Solfeggio music of 432 Hz. Let the music become once again a tool to raise human nature and a method to connect you with Source.

The Gregorian chant is named after Saint Gregory the Great, who was pope from 590-604. The music, which is relatively simple, yet also complex, was and still is sung in Catholic churches and monasteries around the world by the monks and the nuns during services and throughout their day. They sing without accompaniment and chant prayers from the words of the sacred texts.

The chants are not for the individual singing them, though, but rather they are prayers on behalf of all humanity. These musical beginnings have not been a part of my experience, but I mention them here because they are found to be some of the highest vibrational music and should be researched further.

Sanskrit Chants. Sanskrit has long been called the language of vibration, and it has been a major influence in my life.

Your mind becomes quiet by singing the Sanskrit vibrational sounds, and you often feel a sense of peaceful connection with everything. Scientists tell us that everything in the universe is made up of the vibration of atoms and molecules. To come in contact with a language of vibration is to come in contact with essentially what we truly are. Beyond that, when you connect with what you truly are on the physical level, you can more easily feel what you are beyond the physical, or who you are as a spiritual being.

An interesting aspect of applying Sanskrit chants to your life is the unique way they influence our growth. Each person will have their own unique experience. The more you use them, the more inner stillness you will find. Inner stillness gives you access to a feeling of being more connected spiritually, and therefore less alone in a world of challenges.

The easiest way to begin chanting Sanskrit chants is to start by chanting "Om." Om is not just a sound — it's a wave of the universe. It is a powerful sound that lies within us. Chanting Om is a sacred practice that energizes our body, raises mental awareness, calms the stomach, reduces anxiety, supports the immune system, and lowers blood pressure. Om connects all living beings to nature and the Universe, and you can chant it aloud or silently to yourself.

- Find a comfortable place to sit, with your spine straight and your ears aligned with your shoulders and your hips.

- Take three deep gentle breaths in through your nose and out slowly through your mouth to calm your mind and relax your body.

- Now take a deep breath in, choose a note that feels comfortable to you, and allow the word Om to emerge slowly out through your voice. This vibration is usually felt low in your abdomen. Continue the sound as long as your breath will allow, and as you finish the word bring your lips together with an extended mmmmmm... which brings the vibration up into your head.

- Take another deep breath, and repeat.

- You can repeat this process just a few times, or for an extended period of time possibly 5-10 minutes

- When you complete your practice, sit in stillness and notice the way your body and mind responds to this Sanskrit chant.

Another common chant is the Chant of Compassion. It is also called the 6-word or 6-syllable Chant. Each syllable has a healing vibration for different areas of the body. Here are the words, their phonetic pronunciations, and their meanings:

Om (Oh.....mmm) = the foundational sound of the universe

Mani (Mah nee) = jewel; symbolizes the pure nature of our heart, compassion & love

Padme (Pahd may) = lotus; symbolizes wisdom and beauty coming out of difficulty

Hum (Hum) = indivisibility; symbolizes the power of unity with all

The words are all connected together in the chant as one continuous word — om-mani- padme-hum

- Find a comfortable place to sit with your spine straight and your ears aligned with your shoulders and your hips.

- Take three deep gentle breaths in through your nose and out slowly through your mouth, to calm your mind and relax your body.

- Now take a deep breath in, choose a note that feels comfortable to you, and allow the words Om Mani Padme Hum to emerge from your voice. (Do not extend the syllables, let them all merge together.)

- With one breath, you might be able to repeat the chant multiple times.

- When your breath runs out, take another deep breath, and repeat.

- You can repeat this process just a few times, or for an extended period of time, possibly 10-15 minutes

- When you complete your practice, sit in stillness, and notice the way your body and mind respond to this Sanskrit chant

What music resonates with you? Have you used any of the highest frequency music we have suggested? Your health and level of consciousness is our business, and we are grateful to assist you in this way.

And the Beat Goes On

Research demonstrates that listening to "healing beat" music can result in mental and physical relaxation. Healing beat music has a tempo that is synchronized with the person's heart rate. When the beat of music is harmonious to nature, it will be healing to our bodies.

I share how the beat of music has affected me, even in my sleep, and offer my own system to determine how the music I am listening to is affecting me that you, too, can use:

- How does your body feel?

- What emotions does it elicit?

- Does it make you want to move?

When I was in high school, my morning alarm was set to music. When the timer went off, it was not an alarm that blared, but instead the music from the local pop station. While that would not be comforting to me now, at the time I recall many a morning when I would literally wake up ready to dance. I studied drumming early in my elementary years, and the beat of the music lit me up, even in my sleep. Even now, when the beat is strong, I can dance the night away. My body takes on a life of its own, and it is nearly impossible to calm it down.

Music affects us physically. Our heartbeat, respiration, and brain waves all synchronize with different rhythms. Slow music tends to slow down our heart rate, respiration and brain waves. Fast music has the opposite effect, tending to speed us up. The field of music therapy has developed the use of music and musical interventions to restore emotional, physical, and spiritual health and well-being. Music therapists use sound vibration to focus on mental and emotional support, such as improving communication skills, decreasing inappropriate behavior, improving academic and motor skills, increasing attention span, strengthening social and play skills, pain management, and stress reduction. Music therapy can also help individuals on their journey of self-growth and understanding.

A review of the research related to music and physical exertion concluded that music with an appealing beat provides:

- a reduction in the feeling of fatigue

- an increase in levels of psychological arousal

- a physiological relaxation response

- an improvement in motor coordination

Steps and Methods

Here is what you can do:

With the chosen music playing at moderate volume, take a body inventory again. This time, feel into the general feeling of your body as a whole. You can grade yourself on a scale of 10, with 1 being very relaxed, and 10 being very tense. Anything above 5 or 6 is actually detrimental to your health, and your body will begin demonstrating symptoms of ailments, if it hasn't already.

How does the music make you feel from a mental/emotional

standpoint (on a scale from 1, being blissful, to 10, being highly anxious or highly depressed)?. Again, any grade above a 5 or 6 causes you distress in your body and your mind.

Does it provoke a desire to move with the music? This is my ultimate litmus. I used to wake up to music on the radio. My favorite music was the songs that made me want to dance right out of bed in the morning. If it makes you want to get up and move — it is good for the soul.

There is rhythm in all of life. Selecting music with a rhythm that entrains to nature will also entrain to your heartbeat and your brainwaves. My hope is that you have gained an understanding of how music — and its rhythm — can ignite healing during health challenges. You get to decide. Choose music that resonates with your soul, and it will also resonate positively for your health.

How does this information resonate with you? Have you taken the time to really feel into your body's experience?.

Music and Your Mind

Many people are unaware of how powerful music is and how it impacts brain development and behavior. Here, we will explore the benefits of music on behavior. I will tell you a story of my Mom's reasons for enrolling me into learning to play an instrument, and also provide you support for the following ways you can enhance your own mental abilities with music:

- Play classical music in the background throughout your day.

- Add Mozart or Baroque music during times of learning.

- Learn to play an instrument.

- Make a song out of your lessons.

- Enroll in music therapy.

By adding some of these activities to your daily routine, you can support your brain health and enhance your emotional well-being.

When my sisters and I were young, my mom made it a point for each of us to learn to play a musical instrument. My first choice was to learn to play the drums. I'm not sure that would have been my mother's first choice, but she allowed the situation to play out. The deciding factor for changing my choice came when I had to carry a drum back and forth to school — and it was heavy. I settled on learning the clarinet.

Though I did not ever perceive myself as very good, I continued playing in the band through college, and it was always the foundation of my social life. I give my mother credit for enduring the early years of squeaks and squawks in order to gain the benefits that playing an instrument provides.

What can you do to increase your mental abilities, and the abilities of those in your family?

Steps and Methods

Add classical music in the background throughout your day. For the unborn child, classical music, played at a rhythm of 60 beats per minute, equivalent to that of a resting human heart, provides an environment conducive to creative intellectual development, according to Dr Thomas Verny in his book The Secret Life of the Unborn Child (1982). Research is also showing that learning potential can be increased a minimum of five times by using 60 beats per minute music.

When studying, have Mozart or Baroque music playing in the background. The power of music to affect memory is quite intriguing. Mozart's music and Baroque music, with a 60 beats per minute beat pattern, activate the left and right brain. When the left and right brain are activated simultaneously, learning and retention of information is increased. The information being studied activates the left brain while the music activates the right brain.

Learn to play an instrument. Preschoolers who studied piano performed 34% better in some forms of reasoning ability than preschoolers who spent the same amount of time learning to use computers, as reported by Rauscher and Shaw, in Neurological Research, February 1997.

And activities that engage both sides of the brain at the same time, like playing an instrument or singing, increases the brain's ability to process information.

Make a song out of your lessons. Ancient Greeks sang their dramas because they understood how music could help them remember more easily.

Honor your brain by continuing to keep it active. Using these simple ideas can provide many benefits now and in your more mature years.

Chapter 12

Our Significant Connections

We need each other. How we interact with each other can make the difference between a happy or an unhappy life. But relationships are complicated.

In fact, relationships can seem quite complicated until you realize that they serve a purpose in the spiritual realm. They teach us about ourselves. They teach us about each other. They teach us forgiveness, caring, empathy, and love.

Each relationship we encounter or are engaged in long term is either teaching us something we need to learn or is encouraging a shift in our path. This is what we're exploring here: How relationships teach us something we need to know about ourselves.

It is the spiritual "job" of our close associates to mirror back to us the very things that are out of balance with us and to assist in guiding us along our spiritual growth path. The methods employed are almost never straightforward, and, if they are, for some reason we often fail to get the obvious message.

Andy Crouch writes in his book, Culture Making (2013), that God created a world "designed for the flourishing of exquisitely relational creatures, male and female, who themselves are very good because they bear the image of a relational God."

It is true, we are meant to be in a relationship with another. However, it may be for other reasons than you have commonly understood.

Here, we will explore the meaning behind the scriptures' guidance to pursue a significant relationship. I will share my personal experience with a short-term marriage, what I know now that I didn't know then, and we will identify the underlying messages behind some of the ways our relationships guide us, such as:

* Resist the temptation to make it about them.

- Accept the idea that it IS about you.

- The Universe works for us, not against us.

- Seek counsel from your higher self.

As long as we are safe, it truly doesn't matter what relationship we are in. All relationships are there to teach us what we need to know for the elevation of our consciousness. My hope is this information will in some ways take the pressure off if you are searching for your perfect mate, and in some ways help you to take the responsibility that is truly only yours in developing the meaningful relationship you seek.

I waited until I was 30 years old before getting married. I waited that long partly because I was pursuing my career, and because my parent's divorce when I was a child had been so devastating to me. Then I watched my mom go through three additional marriages before she "got it right." I realized two disturbing realities from that: One was that I did not have a good example of what a relationship should look like, and, Two, I did not want to go through what she had been through.

My relationship developed quickly once we connected, and within nine months we were married. I was like many other people in believing that our love would last, and we could work through the difficulties because our love was so strong. Unfortunately, also like many other couples, shortly after the wedding, our relationship problems began. I created a long mental list of all the ways my husband wasn't doing his part to nurture our relationship — long working hours, many nights out with his buddies, not helping around the house.

But the truth was that from the very beginning neither of us communicated from our hearts. We were addressing each other from our egos. Neither one of us was equipped to deal with a loving relationship because neither of us knew what love was. It was years before I ever had an experience of real, true love, and it was able to occur only because the layers of pain that were stored in my body had slowly been peeled away and the "new" me was no longer living through pain. I had a newfound belief and love in myself, which enabled me not only to feel love, but to be it.

Steps and Methods

Relationships seem quite complicated until you realize there is a purpose for them in the spiritual realm. Each relationship is either teaching us something we need to learn or encouraging a shift in our path. A relationship always teaches us something we need to know about ourselves. Here are some steps to simplify this learning process:

Resist the temptation to make it about them. It is so easy when our spouse, partner, significant other, workmate, or other close person in our life is doing something upsetting to point the finger at them and blame them for "doing something to us." The first thing I share with my clients is that they are not doing anything to you, they are just doing it, and you happen to be the recipient, even if it looks and feels like it is directed at you.

Accept the idea that it IS about you. I know it may not seem that it is about you, but I assure you that it actually is, in some way. Even if the person you are with is abusive, their abuse is on them, of course, but the fact that you are not loving yourself enough to leave is on you. My husband and I divorced because in my mind he was unfaithful. I learned years later after doing significant inner work that I was unable to allow love in. So what could he do, if I couldn't let him love me? He had to go to another who could receive his love.

Yes, I looked like the victim according to society's rules. But over the course of time I could no longer blame him for my inability to receive love. That was the deep reason for the forgiveness. His actions were showing me in the only way he knew, that I needed to allow love in my life.

The Universe works for us, not against us. This was not a conscious decision on the part of my husband. Our higher selves are responsible for the big-picture circumstances, and our conscious mind is usually unaware of the "big why" behind situations. The Universe is always working for you, not against you. Regardless of the nature of the situation, there is always a spiritual reason behind it. Our role is to determine the blessing or the lesson behind the situation.

Meditation also helps you to learn a great deal about any situation.

Here is the technique I use regularly to get answers in meditation:

Before you begin the actual technique, take some time to settle into a state of calm:

- Sit in a comfortable position, feet on the floor, your hands on your lap, facing up to receive or facing down to feel grounded. Be certain your spine is straight.

- Take three deep, gentle breaths in through your nose and out through your mouth. With each exhalation, allow your body to relax even more.

- Say a prayer inviting your personal spiritual connection to be with you during this important experience. "Dear God/Jesus/Allah/Mother Mary/etc., please come to be with me during this awakening experience to guide, protect, and support me. Thank you."

- With each of the next four breaths, release another aspect of your consciousness, until you get to your highest frequency self, or your God-self.

- Breathe in, and when you exhale, say in your mind, 'I release my conscious self, and feel a release.'

- Breathe in, and when you exhale, say in your mind, 'I release my subconscious self, and feel the release.'

- Breathe in, and when you exhale, say in your mind, 'I release my unconscious self, and feel the release.'

- Breathe in, and when you exhale, say in your mind, 'I release any other aspect of my unconscious mind that is between me and my higher self, and I feel the release.'

- Breathe in your highest self, your God-self, and feel your expansion and possibly the quickening of your cells.

- Ask the question regarding your current situation and the message or blessing that is there for you.

- Be available for the answer in whatever way it comes. It can come in as a picture in your mind's eye, or as a thought, or as words that you can hear, or just as a knowing.

- Be sure to clarify anything you don't understand.

- Once you get your information, say a prayer of gratitude for the support and information.

While we all want to be in a relationship with a person we are attracted to and who treats us with respect, there is not just the one out there. My hope is you have gained some wisdom to help you understand and navigate any troubled waters you may encounter in your significant relationship. If you are seeking one, my hope is that this will give you some foundational information that you may need to get started.

Have you ever spent time learning how to interpret dreams? One of the first things you learn is that every person in the dream represents you in some way. The funny thing is, life is nearly the same. Whatever we are experiencing is etherically intended to assist us in our own evolution. Whatever is happening in our life is a reflection of our own inner expressions that need to be addressed in some way.

The Universe gives us clues in a lot of ways, and we don't always listen and receive those messages in a productive manner. I found that I was still holding a significant amount of angst related to my marriage that had ended some years prior. Signs appeared that I needed to work on forgiveness for this particular situation, though they were subtle clues, and I was not paying attention closely enough.

My marriage had dissolved more than 15 years earlier, and for some reason, a picture of my ex was on my kitchen table when I got home from work one day. I didn't know where it came from, and I certainly didn't put it there. I gave it no more thought. A couple weeks later, a girlfriend was moving her office. The building she was originally in was owned by another girlfriend, and I volunteered to help girlfriend 'A' move.

When I pulled up in front of the building where she had her office, there on the porch stood girlfriend A; girlfriend B, who owned the building; and — my ex-husband, whom I hadn't seen or spoken with in 15 years. I got out of my car, walked up to the porch, and hugged all three of them, and proceeded inside. This was another sign I should have paid attention to.

Just a few weeks later, I was scheduled to officiate at my nephew's wedding. The wedding was taking place about an hour-and-a-half drive from me. The morning of the wedding, I went down to the river to meditate. Upon finishing a wonderful meditation, and feeling at peace and refreshed, I walked back from the river to my car. My plan was to go back home, pick up all my items, take a shower, clean up, and head to the wedding early. That is not what happened. On my way back to my car, I realized I didn't have my keys.

No problem, easy solution. I went back down to the river, looked all over the place for my keys and still couldn't find them. My car was locked and I couldn't get in, so what should I do? At that time I wasn't worried, since there was still plenty of time. In my town, you can call the police and they will open up your car for you. That's what I did. I thought maybe I had locked my keys inside the car, but indeed the keys were not there. I convinced the patrolman to take me back to my house to get my second set of keys.

When I got home, I had no idea where my second set of keys were, so I looked around but couldn't find them. I decided I could have the officer take me to rent a car. This was going to be easier than finding my second set of keys. I was getting nervous about making it on time for the wedding. I shared my anxiety with the car-rental clerk, who said, "We'll get you into a car right away. I just need your driver's license and your credit card."

I handed them over, she looked at them, recorded what she needed to, and handed them back. And then a concerned look came over her, and she said, "Ma'am, your driver's license is expired. I'm sorry, I can't rent you a car, or I'll lose my job." My birthday was just two days before, and even though the Department of Transportation gives you 60 days beyond your birthday to replace it, the rental place was strict.

The blood left my face, my stomach balled up, I was in a panic, and I started to cry. I had to get to that wedding, so I called my sister. And for the first time ever, her husband answered the phone. He could tell I was upset, and he asked what was going on. I gave him the short version.

My brother-in-law asked where I was, so he could come pick me up. When I told him, he said, "Isn't that where your ex-husband works?" The car rental place is inside a car dealership. My ex-husband was the finance manager for this car dealership. I asked if he was there. And he was. When he came to the waiting area, I told him the situation. He said, "No problem," and had a car there, no questions asked.

In a state of complete gratitude, I made my way home, got myself together, and headed to the wedding, which I made with moments to spare. This situation had been another sign that there was something I needed to address regarding my ex-husband.

I knew I needed to work on forgiveness. So a few days later, I returned to the dealership late at night when everything was closed. Nobody was there. I just wanted to be present with the energy of my ex. I sat in my car and went into meditation with a request to the Universe, "What am I supposed to be learning from this situation?" Immediately, the message of my husband's role in my life from a spiritual standpoint was crystal clear. His role throughout my life has been to try to teach me how to love myself more. Forgiveness became easy because I understood the big-picture role my ex played in my life.

Every person has a deep meaning for us in our lives that serves us in our consciousness elevation. Look at your relationships. Why are they playing out the way they are? Figure it out before you are forced in a difficult way, like I was, to take a look. Look at your relationships and learn from a spiritual standpoint, what it means for you and your evolution.

Seek counsel from your higher self, asking what their role is in my developing consciousness. When you are in a difficult situation that you don't understand, it is always wise to ask the highest aspect of yourself, your God-self. Once you get the message your higher self is trying to get to you, the situation resolves quite easily and you will not need "the brick."

Meditation also helps you learn about any situation. You can find my suggestions for meditating in the previous section.

Blaming is a common outcome when there are relationship issues. Each person blames the other for their perceived wrongs. Every time we judge another person, we are actually judging the very thing in us that we don't like in them. It is almost always true: We are blaming the other person for our own imbalances. As I unfolded this understanding, it has given me great tools to use in all my relationships.

- Agree whether you believe it or not, that when you are disliking something your partner or friend is doing, it isn't about them — it is always about you. I've heard it said, "You spot it, you got it." That could have a variety of meanings, but in this case it means, 'If you are bothered about something, it isn't about them, it's about your perception of the situation.'

- It is also nearly never really about the thing you are bothered about; instead, it is about how you are feeling about how you related to a similar story in your past.

- Give "them" grace for being the derelict that they are, while also giving yourself grace for blaming them for their inadequacies.

- Do an inner inventory to uncover your own areas where you are lacking self-love.

- Establish relationships with the type of people YOU want to be.

- Become the person you want to be around.

The Universe is set to assist you in helping you evolve. My attempt with this information is to illustrate the possible manner in which you may receive divine messages, and how you can assist in your life's evolution.

Your path is not only vitally important to you, but it is also significant for the evolution of the planet. How does this resonate with you? Place your ideas in the comments below. Others may benefit from your wisdom as well.

How Are You Relating to You?

Your most intimate relationship is the relationship that you have with yourself.

I spent years not knowing who I was. I knew who I thought I needed to be to fit in, but had no real concept of the real me. I wore a mask to hide who I really was from myself and from others.

Your most intimate relationship must be with yourself. Take the necessary time and work with the necessary people to uncover the most authentic, most real, most beautiful you. When you do, everything about your life will begin to shine. When you are able to absolutely accept yourself and become comfortable in your own skin, it won't matter what others think.

Nobody has life completely figured out. When we are okay with our inadequacies, everyone else will be comfortable with them, too. And our life will become free. We will feel the sense of freedom that is unmatched in comparison to what we've experienced before.

A lack of self-love leads to every argument, every war, and even every suicide. The lessons we learn early on about not being self-centered or self-absorbed are correct if they are discussing these ideas as they relate to an ego standpoint. However, there is nothing more important than to love oneself fully. A lack of love of self is detrimental to spiritual growth and prevents us from achieving our highest potential.

Steps and Methods

Here are the steps I used to dig myself out:

Realize that your brain is not telling you the truth. It is just repeating what it has heard others say about you, or what you have said about you, due to how you felt others thought about you. The liar in your brain has a mission to repeat everything it hears, over and over and over, chattering in the background. It is convinced it is helping you, but it is keeping you stuck in a cloud of discontent, dissolution, and depression.

The liar is fear in disguise, and its voice sounds so much like your own that you believe it is your logical mind thinking. The messages coming from the Liar are usually consistent, and they repeat like scratched records, playing tunes like:

- I can't do this, I can't do that.

- I am not good enough, or smart enough.

- I am not beautiful enough, and do not deserve love.

- No one wants to hear what I have to say.

- No one in my family has ever had money, so why should I?

- My life is a mess, and everyone else has it together.

This noise is not true. Your authentic mission is to catch the Liar when it is chattering, and stop the chatter in its tracks by proclaiming out loud, "This is not true!" Then give examples out loud of ways that demonstrate it is not true. This proves to your Liar and also to you what is true.

Each time you catch your Liar and repeat this process, you will help stop the ongoing chatter.

Diligently peel back the layers of childhood trauma. You can do this just as I did by nurturing the little you that experienced each trauma and was never supported or loved in the manner necessary to prevent storing that inner pain. You can say the things the "little you" needed to hear and provide the kind of loving support the little you needed to experience:

- "See" the little you in your mind's eye wherever he or she is, or just pretend they are there.

- Approach them gently. Often they do not trust adults, since, after all, adults are the ones who have disappointed them .

- Develop rapport with them by sending a wave of love from your adult heart to their little heart. Love is the most powerful healer, so keep it flowing into their heart.

- Begin saying what they (you) always needed to hear. All this can be telepathically or out loud. They are very good at hearing either way. Say things such as:

  - I am here for you.

  - You don't have to be alone anymore — I am here with you.

  - I'm sorry you have been hurting for so long. I am here to share your burdens. I can take them, if you want me to.

- You are so strong for holding on for so long. I'm here now.

- You are so important and so loved.

- You are safe now; no one is ever going to hurt you again.

- Do you want to share something that is in your heart? I want to always know what is in your heart.

- You don't have to do anything to be loved; I love you just for being you.

- When they are "ready," bring them into your heart and hold them tight. Let them know how loved they are through your amazing embrace. Hold them until they feel it thoroughly.

- Ask them what they want now. And follow through on their requests.

- For the next few weeks, pretend that you have an invisible friend that just wants to be loved. Tuck them in at night. Wake them up in the morning. Take them for ice cream. Take them to the park to play.

- Focus on feeling and showing them love, joy, and bliss.

- When their love-cup is completely filled, they will reintegrate back into the adult you, bringing with them their playfulness, an empowerment of the true self without the weight of the shadow beliefs.

When you follow this process, long-stored emotions will dissipate, and the emotional triggers will no longer be present. This is called doing your inner work.

Make a pact with yourself that you will not ever say negative things about yourself out loud to others ... or even to yourself, even if you are kidding. Your inner soul hears everything you say and think. Oftentimes, when we say negative things about ourselves, we are merely repeating something we heard from someone else, usually a parent or prominent adult in our lives, or from the Liar in our brain. Regardless of where it originated, these statements are not true, and saying them will cause further underlying emotional disturbance in your life. Self-deprecating humor is damaging in the short term and in the long term. Catch yourself and correct it every time.

Fill your brain daily with positive statements about yourself. You must feed your brain daily to change the repeating patterns of negative self-talk. I have created what I call my Personal Manifesto. This is a recording I have made of me talking about how great I am. I put high frequency music behind it and listen to it all the time. For the first few months after I created it, I listened to it every morning and every evening. It takes 21 days to change a pattern, and I wanted to be sure my pattern of listening to the Liar in my brain was stopped for good.

Here are some of the statements I used in my Personal Manifesto (you are welcome to use these or create some of your own, or both):

- I am a powerful creator with divine and unlimited potential. There are no limits to who I can become and what I can achieve.

- I trust in God and feel His direction in my life.

- I stand tall and strong with a clear vision of who I am and where I am headed.

- I am a confident and charismatic leader, and people are instantly attracted to me.

- I lead with vision and power, and inspire and motivate those around me.

- I live a happy, relaxing, and loving life.

- I continually seek to grow and to learn meaningful truths, so I can become my best self.

- I am an excellent communicator and teach with power, sincerity, and persuasion.

- I attract wealth and prosperity in unlimited abundance. Money comes easily and frequently to me.

- I am in perfect health, and I am filled with energy and power. I have clear goals and move steadily toward achieving them.

- I radiate joy and peace.

- I have a powerful and calm influence.

- I am courageous and fearless, and I like to accomplish hard things.

- I am grateful for today, for right now.

- I find joy in the simple things

Our lives are so filled with distractions, we often spend our entire lifetimes not doing the important work we came to do in this life.

The highest level of our work, and the work that completes our greatest mission, is learning to love ourselves, even under the most difficult conditions.

Chapter 13

The Different Levels of Consciousness

We aren't always efficient. We're not machines. We can't work tirelessly. We need sleep.

But how much? How deep? How often?

One of the ways of achieving more, and gaining more control of our lives, is through sleep and brainwave activity. Here you'll learn about these different brainwave states, including gamma, beta, theta, alpha, and delta.

Our contemporary lives are packed to the brim with so much activity that it's nearly impossible to quiet our minds, even when we are trying to get some sleep. We spend so much time in a heightened state of consciousness, we may not even realize there is another option.

Here, we explore different levels of brainwave patterns and how they affect you. I will share a story of how my brain and the brains of all children work when we are young, and we will expand on the following pointers of how you can stay in the most peaceful brainwave states so you can be most productive and get deeper, more restful sleep:

- Develop a routine of daily meditation.

- See yourself as a spiritual being first, and a human doing, second.

- Do your concentration work earlier in the day.

You may have heard that children learn so easily because their brainwaves spend so much time in the alpha level. You might be familiar with the different levels of brainwaves: theta, alpha, beta, delta, and gamma. Children absorb information all the time in that alpha state.

When I was a child, my parents liked to play games with my two sisters and me that would help enhance our thinking and our minds. My favorite was called The Memory Game. It features cards with pictures on them. Each picture is represented twice in the cards. We spread out the cards on the floor. Then we arranged them face-down in a rectangular pattern of columns and rows. Each person would take turns turning over two cards, trying to get a match. If the cards didn't match, they turned them back upside down, and the next person would have their turn. If the cards did match, you got to continue gathering matches until your two cards did not match.

I loved this game because once a card had been turned over, I could remember where it was, so when the match showed up, I knew where to find the original card. I was a regular winner of this game, even against my parents. Of course, that made me feel really good. But my parents would often want us to play with them separately. In particular, they would sit me out because I won so often. This gave my sisters a chance to practice their mind skills and to be successful.

When I was not playing this game, I'd bounce up and down on a little horse on springs, watching the others play. I was a very active child, and even while I was bouncing up and down on the toy horse, with the television on, and whatever else was going on in the house, or moving and jumping and bouncing and there were distractions, I was still absorbing in this alpha state that was allowing me to take in the entire picture — actually, not just take it in, but remembering the details that went along with it.

Here are the brainwave levels in awakened states:

- Gamma is a state of deep concentration, such as while I'm writing this book and really thinking hard. Its frequency is usually around 30-40 Hz.

- Beta is a state of anxious activity, which is the state of a typical adult human during waking hours. It is the state that most of the brain is in when we have our eyes open and are listening and thinking during analytical problem solving, judgment, decision making, and processing information about the world around us. In this state, learning is more difficult, though it is capable of relaxation. The hertz level is 12-35.

- Alpha is a very relaxed state with a passive attention that is very open to learning. When Alpha predominates, most people feel at ease and calm. Alpha appears to bridge the conscious to the subconscious. It is the major rhythm seen in normal relaxed adults, age 13 and up. Alpha is one of the brain's most important frequencies, to learn and use information taught in the classroom and on the job. You can increase alpha by closing your eyes, or deep breathing, or decrease alpha by thinking or calculating. The Hertz level is 8-12.

- Theta is a state of deep meditation and inward focus, as well as deeper sleep. It is seen in connection with creativity, intuition, daydreaming, and fantasizing, and is a repository for memories, emotions, sensations. Children up to age 13 spend much time in this state. Theta waves are strong during internal focus, meditation, prayer, and spiritual awareness. It is a creative state, yet can be limited in focus. It is a very relaxed state, one able to connect to the wisdom of the Universe. Its frequency is 4-8 Hertz.

- Delta brainwaves are below 4 Hz and occur in deep sleep. Babies up to age one spend most of their time in this frequency. We increase Delta waves in order to decrease our awareness of the physical world. We also access information in our unconscious mind through Delta. A slow brain is a receptive brain to the wisdom of the Universe. A fast brain is a closed mind. Deep sleep is possible in Theta state. Medium sleep is possible in Alpha state. Disturbed sleep is possible in Beta state. Gamma will keep you awake all night.

Steps and Methods

Here is how you can achieve Theta or at Alpha:

Develop a routine of daily meditation. We all need a method to quiet the mind and reduce the input. Some people think watching television or movies is relaxing. While the brain is not really working during these activities, it is still absorbing and processing. Typically, watching television is spent in a mindless absorption state, the Alpha state, and this is dangerous.

Children and adults need a daily routine for quieting the mind, and disconnecting from the stress of constant stimulation. You can do this in the following ways: Add gentle music that does not have words, to help eliminate other distractions, or you may do this without music. It is even more beneficial to take this time outdoors to receive the benefits from nature, as well.

The Inner Eye Candle

- Get a column candle that will be safe to burn while you have your eyes closed.

- Place the lit candle on a table about a foot from your eyes.

- Sit comfortably with your spine straight & your ears over your shoulders & hips.

- With your eyes open, gently focus on the middle of the flame of the candle.

- Watch it with great focus for a minute.

- After about a minute, allow your eyes to gently close. And focus on the image of the candle that remains in your inner eye.

- When your mind wanders, say to yourself, "Thank you for the thoughts, I am with my God/Jesus/Allah/Buddha/etc. now." And bring your mind back to the image of the candle in your inner eye.

Work on relaxing the way you perceive experiences. As we allow ourselves to perceive experiences in a more positive light, our emotions never reach a peak high or a peak low, and therefore our stress hormones remain more in balance.

The Body Relaxation Meditation. We can calm all our thoughts and relax the areas where we feel tight. Use this Body Relaxation Meditation, where you use your breath and your thoughts to produce relaxation in your body (if you feel discomfort anywhere, spend extra time relaxing those areas):

- Sit in a comfortable position, feet on the floor, your hands on your lap, facing up to receive or facing down to feel grounded. You may also do this laying down flat on your back, without a pillow (if you are not so tired that you will fall asleep in the middle of it).

- Take three deep, gentle breaths in through your nose and out through your mouth. With each exhalation, allow your body to relax even more.

- Imagine your focus is a scanner that slowly focuses on and relaxes individual areas of your body. With each exhale, now focus specifically on relaxing the body area of your focus. Exhale three times for each body part, relaxing that area even a little bit more.

- Start at the top of your head and scan your whole head. Relax all the muscles of your eyes, around your ears, your jaw, your tongue, the muscles of your scalp. Exhale three times to relax all of these areas even more.

- Then scan your neck, shoulders, arms, and hands. Again, relaxing each area a little bit more with each exhalation. Really focus on the back of your neck and your shoulders.

- Then scan your entire upper torso, front and back, and around your lungs and heart. And relax each area with three exhalations.

- Move down to your lower torso. Feel into the intestines and the reproductive areas. Relax all the areas of your inner organs with each exhalation.

- Move down to your hips and thighs, and then your knees, lower legs, and feet. Relax all the areas of your big muscles, your buttocks muscles, and your upper thigh muscles.

- Move down to your knees and lower legs. On each of three exhalations, relax these areas a little more.

- And then to your ankles and feet, feeling the little muscles of these areas relax a little more with each exhalation.

- Sit in a state of pure relaxation for 5-10 minutes before gradually bringing yourself back into your daily routine.

- To return slowly, begin by gently rubbing your hands together, followed by gently massaging your face, and then massaging all parts of your outer ears between your fingers and your thumbs. Then take three deep, gentle breaths and say a brief prayer of gratitude for the peace that you now feel.

- Return to your day, feeling relaxed, refreshed, and more at peace.

See yourself as a spiritual being, first, and a human doing, second. Incorporate a slower pace in life. This allows for more reflection, and therefore slower brainwaves. Most of us are always doing rather than being. Source wants us to slow down and just be. This gives us the possibility of hearing inner messages coming from Source.

Here is a quick way to take back your life:

To-Do List — Hack to take back your life.

- Put all the things you need to get done on a list.

- Pick out the items you want to do, and will find joy in doing, and put a star next to those items. Be sure to select only the ones that will allow you plenty of time to enjoy your day.

- Say a prayer to your favorite God Source, telling them you will do these items, and the rest is up to them to get done. Believe it will happen, and it does.

- Go about your day knowing everything on your list will get completed perfectly, according to Divine timing. It is always amazing to me how much easier it is to get things done this way. Source can not help unless we ask. Ask, sit back, and watch what happens.

Do your concentration work earlier in the day. It is very difficult to make the jump from Gamma to Delta quickly. If you are working on projects and doing a lot of brainwork in the evening, you are spending time in concentration, which is in the gamma brain waves. Good sleep happens in the Delta brainwaves. If you make a routine to slow down your brain activity in the evening before bed, you will likely be able to sleep more deeply and feel more rested in the morning.

I lived a significant portion of my adult life in a state of peak alert. I also began and ended my day in meditation. I did not know that meditation probably kept me from having a major health crisis.

It is not possible to continue our lives on overdrive without compromising our health, unless we have an outlet. I shared my own childhood story of how my brain and all children's brains work, and we offered a path of how you can stop the "go-go-go" pattern for a more relaxed and productive life and deeper sleep:

- Develop a routine of daily meditation.

- See yourself as a spiritual being, first, and a human doing, second.

- Do your concentration work earlier in the day.

If you were inside your mind, what would you see? Is it a 12-lane highway with multiple entrances and exits? Or is it a winding path in the quiet, calming forest? We are here to guide you on that winding path. Connect with us here.

How Much Sleep?

Sleep has been a widely researched subject for years. There is so much information on sleep available, and yet people are still having trouble getting good sleep.

Here we explore various reasons people are not getting the sleep they need. I share my own method for reducing the amount and improving the quality of my sleep, and I identify what impacts how much sleep you need:

- Our depth of sleep will determine our quality of sleep.

- Relaxation techniques will improve our mental stress and our quality of sleep.

- Reduce body pain and breathing issues to increase the depth and quality of sleep.

- Increase the amount of meditation you do, and lower the amount of sleep you need.

While much can affect your quality of sleep, and therefore the amount of sleep you need, the sleeping tips offered here have proven very effective for me, and applying them will help you as well.

Do we need eight hours of sleep a night? Some people certainly do, but not everyone. Why do we sleep? Our physical bodies do not really need sleep. They are equipped for ongoing, continuous activity without rest. Our heart keeps beating, our blood vessels keep moving blood, our digestion keeps working, even our brain keeps working. You have experienced that if you have ever awoken in the middle of a dream or been around someone who talks in their sleep. So our physical body does not need sleep.

It is a well-known torture tactic employed in war time to the prisoners of war to keep them awake for days. This makes people go crazy, not because the body needs sleep, but because the Spirit needs to release from the body to go out to "play" and reconnect with the higher frequency of Source energy. The amount of sleep we need is determined by a variety of aspects in our life.

I am not a sleep expert and don't claim to be, but this information is based on many years of personal reflection and personal inner exploration.

Steps and Methods

Our depth of sleep will determine our quality of sleep and therefore how much we need. Our Spirit struggles to leave a body that is not fully in REM sleep. Our Spirit must be present in the body if we wake up.

Mental stress plays a significant role in the depth of sleep we can achieve. Actually, it is a two- way street. Stress keeps you from getting good sleep, and lack of sleep makes you process less effectively, so it creates more stress. Even if you aren't up for large periods of time, you're not sleeping as deeply as you normally would, or you are more restless in your sleep. Stress definitely increases the amount of time it takes to get to sleep, and causes people to wake up more frequently in the middle of the night so you are not getting the REM sleep that your mind needs.

Our mental stress is dependent on the quality and frequency of our relaxation techniques. This becomes a vicious cycle.

If we are stressed over anything, we have a hard time relaxing, so then we have a hard time sleeping, which results in us being extra tired, and when we are extra tired, everything seems more irritating, so our stress level is intensified. It is a cycle that must be interrupted.

I was in this space for almost a year, in the past. I had been abruptly and unceremoniously released from my job of 28 years, and everything in my life seemed to come crumbling down as a result. My stress level skyrocketed because I didn't know where the money was coming from to pay my mortgage, my car payment, or other bills. I truly believed I would end up homeless.

When I sat down to meditate, there were only painful ruminating thoughts about my impending future dancing in my head. We call that monkey-mind in the meditation world. And those monkeys were incessantly intense and emotionally cruel. Day after day, month after month I tried to meditate, and the monkeys were going crazy every time. Since I have used meditation for so long to maintain my optimal level of peace and tranquility, without it, I was a mess.

How did I stop it? Normally, I am not one to use guided meditation of any kind to get centered. While guided meditations are helpful to provide a powerful spiritual experience, for my meditations, I like to set an intention to receive information about some question I have, and then drop in with that intention. In those cases, guided meditations can be a distraction. However, in the case of almost a year without being able to drop in normally, I finally succumbed and found breathing meditations from one of my meditation teachers, Kambiz Naficy.

When I began to follow this guided meditation it was astounding how quickly things changed. This is a testimony to the powerful effects of breathing on clearing our mind, and also to the possibilities of guided meditation when our own mind won't settle down. I was no more than five or six breaths in when it triggered a level of emotional release I had never, ever experienced. I began sobbing. The "watcher" in me knew to let it continue. This went on for quite a long time. I was exhausted, yet renewed.

When I opened my inner eye, the dark cloud that had been hovering around me — like the "Pigpen" character in the Charlie Brown cartoon strip — had lifted and the brilliance of light shone around me. My entire emotional landscape had transformed, and my outlook soared. I didn't know what would happen next, but I knew everything would turn out well.

How can you achieve this type of stress release?

- Be open to the possibility that, "This, too, shall pass."

- Get some exercise.

- Go for a vigorous walk. The feel-good chemical release of endorphins can elevate your perspective.

- Get out in nature.

- In a study reported in Mind (world-class academic journal on philosophy; publishes ongoing research about the human mind), 95% percent of people reported that nature changed their mood from depressed, stressed, and anxious to more calm and balanced.

- Do breathing exercises.

- Changing the rhythm of your breath can signal your brain to relax, which slows your heart rate and stimulates the parasympathetic nervous system, which is responsible for the body's "rest and digest" activities (in contrast to the sympathetic nervous system, which regulates many of our "fight or flight" responses). Triggering your parasympathetic nervous system helps you calm down. You feel better and your ability to think rationally can be restored.

Our physical comfort, whether or not we have body pain or breathing issues, also reflects on the depth of sleep we can achieve. When we are in pain, it is nearly impossible to achieve a good night's rest. I suspect this is part of the reason pain medication is used in hospitals. Without rest, healing is delayed because the main detoxifying organ in our bodies, our liver, is unable to do its best work. Prevention is the best medicine to avoid pain. But when pain is present, what is the best management? When I am in pain, here is what I do, and I suggest it can work for you, too:

- Do a gentle range of motion exercises, such as gentle yoga.

- Get professional help with acupuncture.

- Acupuncture is becoming more widely received in the western world and has been used in Eastern medicine for more than 3000 years. Blockages in the meridian system cause a buildup of excessive energy. This results in pain. Acupuncture releases the excess energy, resulting in the healing flow of energy to return.

- Use food as medicine.

- The capsaicin in chili peppers can relieve back and neck pain. Make a powerful inflammation-reducing tea of one teaspoon each: ginger powder, cumin seeds, coriander seeds, and fennel seeds in 1 liter of water. Drink it hot throughout the day.

- Vitamin B12 can relieve nerve and headache pain.

- Boswellia (otherwise known as the essential oil, Frankincense) can be used to reduce joint pain.

- For relief from intense pain, try arnica.

- Arnica, called "nature's ibuprofen," can be found in health food stores as a topical gel.

- Fish oil is reputed to be as effective as NSAIDs (non-steroidal anti-inflammatory drugs) and is safer.

- And I use PrimeMyBody's Body Therapy, 1,000 mg of hemp salve, for muscle and joint pain relief.

The recent resurgence of medical marijuana has changed the face of pain relief. While I believe in the power of cannabinoids for healing and pain relief, I have also witnessed much abuse of this plant medicine and believe that pharmaceutical grade CBD is a safer solution that can easily provide the relief you seek. However, never settle for the grocery store or gas station options. The CBD formulations I recommend come from Quicksilver Scientific (a line of wellness products) and are formulated by a brilliant scientist, Dr. Christopher Shade.

SCAN ME

Natural Pain Relief Options That Really Work		
Concept	Use	How To
Gentle stretching or yoga	Anywhere that feels tight or painful	Follow gentle stretching or yoga videos on the internet; there are many available.
Capsaicin	For back & neck	Season food w/chili peppers or with 1 tsp in cream form
Powerful Anti-Inflammatory Tea	Whole body	One tsp each: ginger powder, cumin powder, coriander powder, fennel powder; boil in one liter water, drink hot throughout day
Vitamin B12	Nerve & Headache	Take high-quality supplement, 2.4 micrograms daily
Frankincense Essential Oil or Extract (40% concentration)	Joint Pain	Apply oil topically, or take 300 milligrams extract orally.
Arnica - nature's ibuprofen (also known at mountain tobacco)	Intense pain	Apply gel up to 3 times daily.
Fish Oil- High quality Omega 3 supplement with EPA & DHA	Muscle & joints, arthritis	Between 500-1200 milligrams EPA & DHA combined or 2 standard 1000 mg fish oil softgels
PrimeMyBody Body Therapy Salve	Muscle & joints	Apply 2-3 times daily over affected area
Pharmaceutical Grade CBD from Quicksilver Scientific	General relief of all pain that really works	Take orally 2-3 times daily, as recommended.
Medical Marijuana	General relief of pain	As prescribed by qualified practitioners. NOTE: My unpopular opinion is that I am not supportive of this due to its addictive nature.

How much meditation we do also plays a huge role in the amount of sleep we need. Meditation slows down brain waves and allows your spirit to connect to Source during the day. If Spirit connects to Source in the daytime, it doesn't need to connect as much at night, so the amount of sleep you need is minimized.

How much meditation replaces how much sleep? One study out of Oregon State University's College of Business found that 10 minutes of meditation replaces about 44 minutes of sleep. This is dependent on many factors, so your results may vary. The easiest way to determine your sleep vs meditation needs is to practice meditation every day, go to sleep at your normal bedtime, and let your circadian rhythms reset themselves naturally. You may find yourself with more hours in the day before you know it.

Quality of sleep is a strong determinant for long-term health. My hope is that you will apply these ideas. These are the ones that have proven very effective for me in getting uninterrupted deep sleep every night. Applying them will assist you, as well.

Depth of Sleep

Good sleep is vital to optimum health, and yet so many people struggle for even one night of restful, quality sleep. Quality sleep includes how long we sleep, how restful we sleep, and the depth of sleep we achieve.

Here we explore the need for deep sleep. I will share a story of my own sleep patterns and provide the following solutions to turn you into sleeping beauty yourself:

- Steps for getting a good night's sleep

- Sleep time preparation

- Establish a nighttime routine

The idea of getting a good night's sleep is difficult for so many people, and yet it is very possible using proven natural methods.

Deep sleep is important for our health, so that our spirit can do its important work in the ethereal realm, taking care of spiritual business and re-energizing with Source. When we're not sleeping deeply, we don't have that time to revitalize with Source. It's been a well-known torture tactic in war times of captured soldiers to be kept awake to torture them. Just a few days of being kept awake, and people begin to go crazy.

Steps and Methods

To improve your sleep patterns, take good care of your health, reduce the stimulation you have in your evening time, and establish a nighttime routine. I sleep through the night every night, and you can, too.

Follow these steps:

- Feed your body nutritious food as much as possible.

- Get 20-60 minutes of mild to moderate exercise 3-5 times weekly.

- Drink a cup of hot water or chamomile tea before going to bed.

- Feed your brain positive stories or affirmations or both before retiring. I read something uplifting for 10-30 minutes before turning out the light. With the light out, in a seated position in my bed, I listen to my personal manifesto on my phone, which sits on the nightstand.

- Connect with your chosen higher power through prayers of gratitude for all the good things that happened during the day (and everything is good, regardless of our human interpretation). Prayers are sending messages to "God."

- Set an intention for your meditative time and sit and listen for messages from Source for 10 to 30 minutes, or more. Meditation is listening for messages from "God." There is a still small voice of Truth that may come through, sharing meaningful messages for you, based on your intention.

- Scoot down under the covers and be gone before the next breath for the remainder of the night.

Dreams

Have you ever experienced a dream that was so real when you woke up out of it you were dazed and confused, wondering if it really happened? Do you dream in color, or is it black and white? Dreams are as important to our evolution as our daytime activity, especially when we learn to make sense of them.

Here we explore some concepts of dream interpretation. I will share one of my dreams and what I came to understand from it, and I will offer explanations of these steps to take to remember and interpret your dreams:

- Set an intention to remember your dream.

- Upon waking, ask yourself, "Where was I just now?"

- Meditate on the possible meaning.

- Listen for the answers.

Once we can achieve quality sleep, we may realize we are remembering our dreams more readily. Dreams are an extension of our daily work and are ways our consciousness works through issues we have going on in our subconscious storage system. They do have significant meaning to our daily lives, if we learn to understand them more easily.

Though I'm not a dream expert (and there are many books out there on dream interpretation), there are different schools of thought in this area, as you may imagine. The most reliable interpreter of your dreams is you. After all, you are living your life. So how do you remember your dreams, and how can you interpret them?

Steps and Methods

Set an intention before you go to sleep that you will remember your dreams in the morning. This intention is important. Each time I have taken a dream class, where I was asked to record my dreams for discussion the following day, I was able to remember them. One of my mentors, David Wilcock, has been recording his dreams for over 20 years, every morning. Through this practice, he has gained tremendous insight into his mission in the world, as well as what is potentially unfolding in his future.

When you first wake up, ask yourself, "Where was I just now?" It is our beta brain's nature to forget our dreams very quickly, so while you are still in Alpha or Theta, it is important to remember. Don't get out of bed until you make a conscious memory of the incidents in your dream.

Journal as much as you can remember before you get out of bed. As you begin the journaling process, more details of your dreams may come to you. Journaling is the only way the details of the dream will stick. There have been times when a dream was so vivid that I was sure I would remember it, and by the middle of the day it had faded to just the basic points. When you journal it, the memory stays more readily, and, of course, you will also have a reference to return to for the details.

Go into contemplative meditation and ask your higher self, "What are you to take away from this experience?" The meaning behind the dream is the important takeaway, but often the dream is filled with idioms and analogies that are difficult to make sense of. For some reason, it is easier for me to make sense of someone else's dream than my own. My intuition kicks in and the answers come, whereas with my own dreams, I think I am too close to it emotionally. Some basic concepts with dreams are:

A. Everyone in a dream is a representation of you. If there are 4 people in your dream with 4 different roles and personalities, they all represent aspects of you that you can learn from.

B. Colors in your dream, regardless of where they are, represent the levels of consciousness you are achieving and/or what chakra levels you have successfully opened. They match the levels of the chakra system, which are indicated in the following chart (next page):

Once we understand the meaning of our dreams, they provide us with helpful information to log the growth of our consciousness.

I invite you to dive into this fascinating area of life.

It is interesting, colorful, confusing, crazy, otherworldly, and wildly entertaining — and it is also filled with vital clues to track your own evolutionary progress coming in from your higher self.

7th	crown	* cosmic conciousness * understanding * enlightenment
6th	3rd eye	* clairvoyance * intuition * psychic senses
5th	throat	* communication * creativity * healing
4th	heart	* love * hope * compassion
3rd	naval	* energy * vitality * desire + power
2nd	sacral	* emotions * sexuality * intimacy
1st	root	* survival instinct * security * grounding

Chart of the Levels of the Chakra System

Chapter 14

Connect to Your Inner Divinity through Meditation

There is a world beyond this one, and you have access to it. Many people still imagine that meditation is the domain of free spirits who enjoy zenning out on a woven grass mat somewhere.

There's nothing 'woo-woo' about meditation. It is a life-altering practice that has been around for millennia, and virtually every spiritual path integrates some form of it. Even if you aren't on a spiritual path, the benefits assist people in every walk of life to attain greater focus, to maintain more peace, and to feel more centered.

I'll provide you with some techniques to calm your mind and drop into a state of peace, and I will expand on these tips and tricks to help you achieve successful meditational experiences:

- Calm the mind.

- Clean the inner turmoil and gradually achieve a state of sus-tained inner peace.

- Connect with Source.

Meditation has become such an important part of my life that, when I am not practicing it for more than a couple of days, I feel disconnected from myself, ungrounded, and out of sorts. The information presented here will serve as meditation hacks to bring you more success in less time. The Universe is primed and wait-ing for you to make this life-elevating connection.

All through my life, physical activity has been important to me. I've always been involved in sports, possibly because it helps keep my mind busy. When I started in my deep spiritual path, it took tremendous discipline and effort to stop my physical activity long enough to meditate. Just sitting quietly was nearly impossible for me.

I learned to sit, but my mind continued to be on high speed, like a revolving door that didn't stop. When I began to study Qigong, our Qigong master, Chunyi Lin told us not to discipline our mind, but to guide our mind gently. I began to just pay attention to what was happening with regard to my thoughts. I would bring my mind back every time I noticed that I was off on another mind tangent. My mind-gathering statement during all my meditations became, and still is today, "Thank you for the thoughts — I'm with my God now." This usually stops that chain of thinking. When the next chain starts up, back to the same gentle statement, "Thank you for the thoughts — I'm with my God now." Over the course of my 16 years of daily meditations, it is impossible to imagine the thousands of times I have made that statement in my mind.

As we are doing our inner work and we gradually release the layers of trauma we have held inside for so long, that's when we're able to actually connect to Source. Prior to that, we pray to Source, but it is more of a deep yearning for a connection. When the dark energy within is lifted, and the light is shining through, we can then actually experience our pure connection with Source. It is no longer a hope — it is an actual feeling of being fully connected. That is when we experience inner peace. When the darkness is lifted and Source is fully felt, your frequency makes an enormous leap upward, and peace happens. And as we find peace, our consciousness also elevates.

Steps and Methods

Meditation has been proven to have many benefits. One is that it was found through Dr. Gary Young's research to increase the body frequency levels by 15 MHz, in one meditation.

Calm the mind. When you close your eyes and begin meditation, you should expect your mind to be busy, easily distracted, and restless. Just because you've chosen to sit and meditate doesn't mean you will suddenly experience uninterrupted calm, in the same way you would never expect to tame a wild horse overnight. The process of meditating is not difficult — maintaining the focus is the difficult part:

- Find a place where you will not be distracted.

- Determine the minimum amount of time you want to meditate. As a beginner, start with 10-15 minutes. For someone more advanced, 30 minutes to an hour is possible. The longer the effort, the greater the rewards.

- Some enjoy having gentle music without words playing in the background. If that is you, turn your music on now.

- Sit with your spine straight, ears aligned with shoulders, shoulders aligned with hips. You can sit in a chair, or cross-legged on the floor on a pillow.

- Close your eyes and take 3 deep, gentle breaths — in through your nose and out through your mouth — relaxing your body more with each exhale.

- Say a prayer inviting your deity of choice (God, Jesus, Buddha, Mother Mary, etc.) to join you in this sacred time.

- Begin your meditation time by placing your focus on one thing. My two favorites are focusing on my breath, or focusing on visualizing in my mind's eye, a full moon in the night sky.

- Continue with your focus. There is only awareness or non-awareness. The moment you realize you're lost in thought, that's awareness, and that's when you return to the object of focus.

- This is all you have to keep doing — return from your distracted thought to breathing, all the time honing your awareness.

- There is no such thing as a good or bad meditation. With perseverance, the periods between awareness and distraction will get longer and longer.

Clean the inner turmoil and gradually achieve a state of sustained inner peace. Sometimes this process will start on its own, as mine did. It's not necessary to take as long as I did. It is more time efficient to start and follow through this process with intention. I will spell out the fast track here for you:

- Identify the core shadow that comes from your painful trauma. The core shadow belief or beliefs are the perceptions of yourself of who you are as a result of the pain. Our original, unhurt self resonates from a pure angel-like perspective without any hurts that taint our belief of who we are. Core shadow beliefs put a stamp on us that makes us feel 'less than' in some way. Some typical Core Shadow Beliefs are:

- There is something wrong with me.

- I cannot trust anyone.

- I'm a bad person.

- I'm not lovable.

- I don't deserve to have what I want.

- Love does not last.

- I am worthless.

- I am never going to be successful.

- Identify the location in your body where that energy was stored. We all have the ability to quiet our thoughts and pay attention to where we feel tightness or discomfort. Sometimes we already have an ailment that is a clue to where we might be storing emotions. To take a body inventory, I like to use the body inventory meditation:

  - Sit in a comfortable position, feet on the floor, your hands on your lap, facing up to receive or facing down to feel grounded. Be certain your spine is straight.

  - Take 3 deep gentle breaths in through your nose and out through your mouth. With each exhale, allow your body to relax even more.

  - Imagine your focus is a scanner that slowly focuses on individual areas of your body to see where there is tightness or discomfort. Pay attention to subtle indications and also to those that are strong.

    ◊ Start at the top of your head and scan your whole head.

    ◊ Then scan your neck, shoulders, arms, and

hands.

◊ Then scan your entire upper torso, front and back, and around your lungs and heart.

◊ Move down to your lower torso; feel into the intestines and the reproductive areas.

◊ Move down to your hips and thighs, and then your knees, lower legs, and feet.

Where was the tightness? Where was the discomfort? Journal all the areas you found in your body that were experiencing tightness or discomfort.

Connect with Source. (Source is the term I use for "God," and I also interchange it with "the Divine," or "the Universe.") How is that connection made?

- We have already mentioned my number one method, which is meditation.

- Other ways include getting out in nature:

  ▪ Breathe in fresh air.

  ▪ Listen to the wind and other sounds.

  ▪ Put your feet on the earth; take in all the beauty and essence of nature.

  ▪ Even meditate out there; just sit and Listen.

  ▪ Drop your feet into a stream as you listen to the water trickle by.

  ▪ Find a park, or some woods (I can be found sitting on the ground in my front yard many days in the summer).

- Spend time really tapping into what you are grateful for; relishing what you are grateful for brings more beauty into your life.

- Every day, notice little miracles and synchronicities, like seeing repeating numbers regularly — life's surprises, like when you are thinking about someone and they call you — and manifestations, like you want some chocolate cake, and your neighbor stops by with just that an hour later, which they just baked.

- Many people journal their thoughts, and often receive spontaneous messages through writing.

- Connect with mystical, magical methods like using a pendulum, crystals, essential oils, or card readings.

- One of my favorite ways to connect is through energy work. I use Qigong and yoga, and there is also Tai Chi, Reiki, Acupuncture, Shiatsu, and others. Check them out to see if there is one you connect with.

Other things you can try: Sound Work, such as chanting, drumming, gongs, crystal bowls, and others — immersing yourself in certain sounds can transport you into a very meditative state. Dancing can also produce a wonderful connection; when you allow your body to lead you where it wants to go, your connection to Source can be found. Massage is another method to bring you into your body fully, and in this state it is easier to make a Source connection.

Anytime you make a connection to Source, you will find yourself in a more relaxed state and things will bother you less, and you will feel more content. You may also be suddenly inspired by thoughts of creativity. The more we connect to Source, the more we may want to distance ourselves from people who are abrasive or negative.

Where would I be without meditation? At rare times when I have not meditated, my day is not complete, my mind is not as focused, my temperament is less steady, and I don't feel my normal state of peace. The information presented here is provided so you will have the foundation to begin a successful practice of meditation. Make a commitment to do it for 10 days. One or two days is not enough to overcome the ego. The energy of the Universe is more supportive for meditation than it has ever been. Start today and see how quickly your consciousness shifts. Contact us at my website and let us know about it.

Frequency of Meditation

The benefits of meditation are many and may vary for each person. Regardless of your meditation mission, embarking on a program with 100% commitment will yield even greater benefits than you may anticipate.

Here we explore diving into the deep end of meditation. Buddha said, "If you don't have time to meditate for 20 minutes, then meditate for an hour." Our lack of time indicates we are filling our life with too much clutter. One of the benefits of meditation is you will realize what is important and what can be eliminated. I will share my own story of stepping into the meditation deep-end, and leave you with tips to assist you in getting the most out of your meditation commitment:

- Make a pact with yourself and one other to initiate a 100-day challenge for meditation.

- Set aside the same time every day, and stick to that time.

- Set up a sacred location that you will always use.

- Put it on your calendar, and honor this appointment before all others.

- Wear the same "sacred" clothes when meditating.

- Use the same music.

- Connect with the same spiritual master.

Dabbling in meditation is helpful and will give you a taste of the possibilities. Diving into an intense meditation routine will bring forth the depth of benefits that are waiting for you to enjoy. Do it. Your life will transform and improve. I promise.

About 16 years ago, I was meditating a few times a week. My morning meditation was filled with struggle, trying to keep my mind under some level of control in order to go into a deeper level of connection, silence, and peace. I was relatively successful, but it was still fraught with much difficulty. My Qigong master, Chunyi Lin, challenged us to do Qigong for a hundred days straight. Our process included standing movements that are more like moving meditation followed by seated meditation. I found when I meditated every single day for a hundred days that everything started calming down more quickly. The struggle I had when meditating just two to four days a week started to diminish. The benefits of the body and mind succumbing to the daily process became easier.

It was much easier to meditate when my body and mind expected it to happen every day. The more details I included in this process, the easier it became. I wore the same meditation clothes each day and did the same routine each day at the same location and at the same time. I stood by that routine so much that even my dog knew it, and if my timing was a few minutes off, she sat on my meditation pillow and barked to call me in. Of course, sometimes "life happened" and I had to change my routine, but staying by it as much as possible did so much for creating a habitual nature for my body, my mind, and my chemistry.

Additionally, the energy in the space I meditated began to elevate. That elevated energy also assisted me to go deeper in meditation. Every aspect of this began to work in my favor toward a deeper, more meaningful meditation experience. This foundation set the stage for daily meditation for many years to come. Though there have been times when I have not been able to get it in, nearly every day I have maintained my routine, and it has always been the most important part of my day. It sets a positive tone for the remainder of the day.

These days, my dog, my cat, and I meditate twice a day. First thing in the morning, after the animals go out and I feed them, we meditate, and it's so habitual that my dog, Mia, who is now 15 years old, still finds her way to my meditation pillow and will bark until I get in there. My cat, Crystal, joins us once I sit down. They know what the plan is.

My second meditation is the last thing before going to sleep at night. We also have a nighttime routine. Drink warm water, get ready for bed, climb in, and sit on my meditation pillow, read something inspirational for a bit, turn out the light, and go into meditation. Those meditations can last anywhere from 15 minutes to an hour or more. When it feels complete, I slide down under the covers and doze off quickly.

Steps and Methods

By doing meditation regularly, you upgrade the experience. Here are some techniques you can use for yourself that have worked for me:

Make the decision that you are going to meditate daily for 100 days. It is easiest if you create a group activity of at least one other, so you can be accountable to each other. Determine the beginning date and set your mind to it. Make a chart or use the calendar to cross off the days. Following each completion, make a big deal about crossing off your day. This may seem like a silly thing, but there is science behind it. Our brain triggers the release of small doses of the feel-good chemical, dopamine, every time we check the box. Our whole system will cooperate better if it receives its dopamine "gift" each day.

Set aside the same time every day and stick to that time. Make it the most important appointment of the day. Regardless of what else may try to sneak in to that time slot, you already have an appointment at that time. For some reason, it is easier to keep an appointment with someone else when we set it, than to keep one for just ourselves. There are so many aspects of life that we can allow to steal our time. This is a boundary you must set. If your day has to start earlier, then get up with enough time that you include your meditation before work, to go along with the other aspects of your morning routine.

Set a sacred location that you will always use. Put a candle and other sacred items on an "altar" in that space to prepare it for its sacred duty. It is helpful to establish the sacred nature of your meditation space. If you have a room you can devote to your sacred time, that is the very best, but it's not necessary. I have converted a space in my open construction home that used to be my dining room. It is where I see clients, and where I meditate daily. As you build the energy in that area through your daily connection to Source, this will assist you in going deeper in your meditation over the course of time

Put this on your calendar and honor it above any other commitment. Even five minutes a day has significant results. I recommend setting aside 30 minutes daily, and ideally, 30 minutes two times daily. Several years ago I did a meditation research study as a part of the requirements for my Masters in Metaphysics degree. During that study, I used the students in my sports medicine class as my study subjects and students in another class across the hall as my control group.

Each group filled out a questionnaire before and after the study. No students in either group were previous meditators. My students did five minutes of meditation at the beginning of each class. Some gentle music was turned on and they were to "look" at a single object in their mind's eye for that five minutes. Every minute or so, I would gently ask, "Where's your focus?" The control group just did their normal daily routine, whatever that was. At the end of the 14-week class, the final questionnaire was completed and the results from the meditation group were stunning. Every single student reported the following:

Having their highest grades that term, more than any other

Feeling less stressed throughout the term

Experiencing better relationships with their friends and families.

Feeling a greater sense of wellbeing

That was just five minutes, three times a week. The results for you will be magnified when you initiate this in your daily routine every day. We don't meditate to be better at meditation — we meditate to be better at life.

Wear the same "sacred" clothes when meditating. The clothes you wear can also assist you in your meditation success. It may seem a bit silly, but even the frequency of your clothes will elevate when you use them for meditation every day. Surrounding your body and your space with high frequency assists in your success. Your body will also respond to the ritual of you putting those clothes on, as well. It will trigger the response of, "Ahhh, start quieting down now, the meditation will begin shortly." This may be the beginning of your meditation ritual, so it will be an important aspect.

Play the same music every time. The exact routine is important. When you use that music to meditate every single time, eventually, whenever you play that music, your body and mind will quiet down. My meditation music does that for me when I am amped up and want to calm down.

When you begin your meditation, say a prayer to the same spiritual guide every time. Invite them to assist and support you and to provide you wisdom. Call them by name. This will assist you in developing a unique bond with that spiritual being. Because I was raised in a Christian environment in my earliest years, I chose to pray to Jesus. I developed a unique relationship, and now it is Jesus who comes to speak to me with special messages. You, too, can speak to and hear from your special guide or guides. Start with just one.

No matter how much meditation you are already doing, I invite you to do more. An intense meditation routine will multiply the benefits you experience, and raise your frequency, the frequency of your home, your neighborhood, and everyone in your path. Get started today and prepare to transform your life and the lives of all those you encounter.

Depth of Focus

While basic meditation has very real benefits, as we continue to maintain our commitment we are exposed to otherworldly experiences that may not be easy to digest or explain. Are you ready to have real experiences from beyond the veil?

Here, we explore what's beyond "the veil" that is available to those with eyes to see and ears to hear. I share a story about one of our techniques from Qigong, and share ways in which my meditation practice expanded, and yours can, too:

- Harness the mind?

- Have laser focus on your meditation mission.

- Reach for your Source connection.

- Maintain your composure, regardless of what appears.

My hope for you is you have a life-changing meditation breakthrough that brings the spiritual realm directly into your heart and mind. Once you do, there is no unknowing of what is true for you or the rest of the world.

In Qigong, we were taught to meditate for one to two hours at a time. This took real dedication. This level of dedication is not for the faint of heart, and is not completely necessary. However, we must get your mind to settle down so you can focus. When we can meditate on a daily basis and regain the experience of deep connection to Source, this is the hallelujah experience, when everything in our life improves.

Steps and Methods

Here are some steps to move you toward deep meditation:

Techniques for harnessing the mind. This is the most difficult aspect, depending on what meditation techniques you use. When the mind is clear of our human beliefs, our human ideas, and our human to-do lists, when it is essentially empty to the unimportant noise of our human existence, then it can be available to the wisdom of the cosmos.

When we think we are our thoughts, we identify with all the noise our thoughts are making. We believe what our thoughts are telling us is true. Then, when those thoughts are of a destructive nature, telling us how unimportant we are, or how ugly we are, or unloved we are, our self-esteem plummets and we become anxious and depressed. Anxiety and depression come from being misaligned with our soul's mission.

You can use the chart (on the next page) to better understand the vast benefits associated with your subconscious and unconscious mind, and how meditation is the best training technique to tap into and even control this incredible power in its deepest way:

- The beginning of harnessing your mind is to stop filling it up with garbage:

  - Reduce or eliminate media that spew garbage at you continuously.

  - Don't engage in the "he said-she said" drama of common conversations. Talk about ideas, not people.

Anatomy Of The Mind: Meditation Gives You Access To Your Mind's Most Powerful Layers

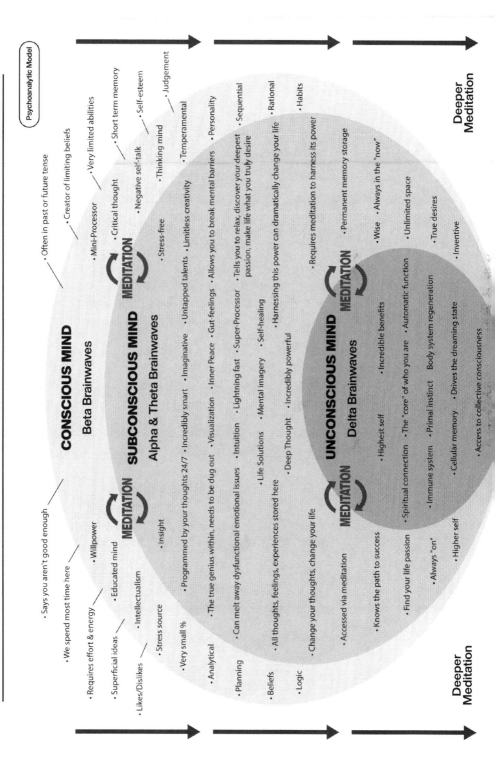

Psychoanalytic Model

CONSCIOUS MIND
Beta Brainwaves

- Says you aren't good enough
- We spend most time here
- Requires effort & energy
- Superficial ideas
- Likes/Dislikes
- Stress source
- Very small %
- Analytical
- Planning
- Beliefs
- Logic
- Willpower
- Educated mind
- Intellectualism
- Insight
- Often in past or future tense
- Creator of limiting beliefs
- Mini-Processor
- Critical thought
- Very limited abilities
- Short term memory
- Self-esteem
- Negative self-talk
- Thinking mind
- Judgement
- Temperamental

MEDITATION

SUBCONSCIOUS MIND
Alpha & Theta Brainwaves

- Programmed by your thoughts 24/7
- Incredibly smart
- Imaginative
- Untapped talents
- Limitless creativity
- Stress-free
- The true genius within, needs to be dug out
- Visualization
- Inner Peace
- Gut-feelings
- Allows you to break mental barriers
- Personality
- Can melt away dysfunctional emotional issues
- Intuition
- Lightning fast
- Super-Processor
- Sequential
- Tells you to relax, discover your deepest passion, make life what you truly desire
- Life Solutions
- Mental imagery
- Self-healing
- All thoughts, feelings, experiences stored here
- Deep Thought
- Incredibly powerful
- Harnessing this power can dramatically change your life
- Rational
- Change your thoughts, change your life
- Requires meditation to harness its power
- Habits

MEDITATION

UNCONSCIOUS MIND
Delta Brainwaves

- Accessed via meditation
- Knows the path to success
- Find your life passion
- Always "on"
- Higher self
- Highest self
- Spiritual connection
- The "core" of who you are
- Immune system
- Primal instinct
- Cellular memory
- Access to collective consciousness
- Incredible benefits
- Automatic function
- Body system regeneration
- Drives the dreaming state
- Permanent memory storage
- Wise
- Always in the "now"
- Unlimited space
- True desires
- Inventive

MEDITATION

Deeper Meditation

Deeper Meditation

- Make a pact with yourself that you will no longer tell lies...even white lies...even "just kidding" lies...even self-deprecating lies. Lies absolutely confuse our soul and require our mind to try to make sense of it.

- The mind is to be of service to you, not the other way around. Be the captain of your ship, and guide your mind toward your desired destination.

- When you are in meditation, gain control over your continuous thoughts. Every time you realize a wandering thought is happening, you can repeat the statement I say to my mind: "Thank you for the thoughts, I am with my God now." Gently bring your mind back to your focus of silence. Repeat it every time you catch your thoughts wandering off again. I have done this many, many times in one mediation in the past. Eventually, your mind realizes you are serious and slows its activity.

- I have found it is easier and more effective to give my mind something to do. In Kriya meditation, we don't need to manage our thoughts because our mind is too busy trying to follow the breath.

  - As you breathe in, listen and pay attention to the breath coming in and flowing down to your lower abdomen.

  - As you breathe out, pay attention to your breath exiting your body.

  - As you breathe in, visualize in your mind's eye that your breath is iridescent, white light flowing in and filling up your entire torso.

  - As you exhale, visualize smoke exiting out of your body, taking any old stored emotions, toxins, or ailments out with it, sending it all into the atmosphere as extra energy you no longer need.

  - Continue following the breath with the same patterns or different patterns, depending on your comfort with this process.

- One of my meditation teachers says to follow the thought as if it is a leaf on the river. This occupies the mind in a gentle way.

- Or you can watch for the next thought (this is an excellent technique). When you sit in anticipation of the next thought, often no other thoughts come. Try it. Just sit in meditation and focus on watching for the next thought as you breathe.

- Continue doing your inner work to clear out the stored emotional trauma that can be producing those negative thoughts in the first place. With every layer of old emotional trauma I have cleared, the noise in my head gets quieter and quieter. The monkey-mind is not always quiet these days, but more often than not, I can sit in quiet meditation without chasing my mind continuously.

Focus on your mission, or the intent of your meditation, and keep your mind in one place. If your mission is to feel more relaxed, keep your mind and body relaxed as you use the steps from above. If your mission is to clear your stored inner emotions, keep your focus on "looking" for emotions that want to bubble up. And when they do, allow them to express themselves until their energy runs out. If your mission is to connect to Source, set your intention and then focus deeply on allowing messages to come in from Source. They will arrive through pictures, words, or thoughts.

Reach for Source connection of mind, body, and spirit. As we climb the scale of consciousness as depicted by Dr. David Hawkins, there are more and more elevated ways we understand the meaning of Source. At the lower levels of consciousness, we think of our God as a vengeful, punishing God. At higher levels of consciousness, we think of our God as a loving and wise God, and at the highest level of consciousness, we completely resonate as an extension of God.

Regardless of the level we are resonating at, it is significant to know that we are never alone. A variety of ethereal beings serve us. All we have to do is send out a request to get responses from Masters such as Jesus, Buddha, Mother Mary, Quan Yin, Krishna, and many more; angels at varying levels, with the closest to us being the Archangels, such as Michael, Uriel, Gabriel, Raphael, Metatron, Ariel, and others; deceased ancestors from your family lineage going back many generations — if you are connected to a tribal lineage, there may be tribe members available.

I have an ongoing conversation with my "ethereal love team," as I call them. They are a part of my daily existence. Others that are available to us are the plant and animal kingdom. Angels will often use animals as messengers, especially birds, as they can travel across vast distances with ease.

You can learn to understand the meaning that these animals symbolize in order to improve your ability to communicate with those in the spiritual realm. Just today, as I was talking with some friends, a hummingbird came and hovered at the window for many seconds. There were no flowers around the area; it was clearly there to deliver a message. The message she gave us is to learn from our past mistakes and then jump back into our current reality to prevent the same mistakes from happening again.

Whenever there is an encounter beyond what might be considered normal, there is a spiritual message. You can check in immediately, or you can check online for the meaning — type "metaphysical meaning of _____" (fill in the blank with the type of messenger that visited you) into the search bar of the Internet, and you will gain the information you seek. My favorite reference for animal encounters is the book entitled Animal Speak (2002), by Ted Andrews.

Do your best to maintain your composure, regardless of what experiences show up during your meditation. In the spiritual realm, there are occurrences that are "normal" to them, but to us humans they may seem amazing, weird, scary, or in some way not normal. You may be brought to experience something like this, and, depending on your reaction, it can become a normal part of your life, or it will be taken away and not return for many, many years, if it ever returns at all.

For example, let's say you are meditating and begin to have clear visions of the future. You may say to yourself, "That is interesting; I can see how I might be able to help with this situation." You will likely continue to experience the gift of prophecy. Or you may freak out in some way, get very excited or emotional, and go around telling everyone in your path what just happened to you in an 'I can't believe it' kind of way. You will likely not experience that gift again for many years, if ever again. Our ethereal team will give us what we are ready for, but not if we are searching for it. We must be available but not hoping, needing, reaching, and wanting for these things to happen. And when they come, we must respond in a way that it is normal and regular, instead of reacting like something out of this world just happened.

Deep spiritual experiences are not just reserved for Tibetan Monks and Indian gurus. The spiritual realm is available to all of us when we demonstrate commitment and willingness to gain that connection. My hope for you is that you experience breakthroughs that bring the spiritual realm before your eyes with real connection. When it happens, you will be forever changed, and there will be no turning back.

What's Out There? Possibilities of Ethereal Connections

You don't have to be a guru to have otherworldly experiences. Paramahansa Yogananda shares some of his other worldly experiences in his book, The Autobiography of a Yogi (1946). He accomplished these ethereal gifts through decades of study with his enlightened guru, and became an enlightened guru himself.

Here, we explore possible experiences available to you. I will share some stories of what happened to me, and to my students, and a few tips on what you can do:

- Gifts that can develop

- Experiences that can happen

- Complete Oneness with Source

While otherworldly experiences should not be the goal of spiritual growth, they may be useful. My wish for you is to seek the highest level of spiritual connection so that you can come to know God/Universe/Source (playfully named GUS) as intimately as I do. There is no greater mission, nor outcome, than making that ultimate connection so that there is no longer a separation between you and Source.

A few years ago, I was planning for a community ceremonial event that I entitled "The Celestial Trifecta" (there was a full moon, an eclipse, and the summer solstice happening at the same time). It was to be held at the Infinite Living Center for Holistic Experiences, which is also my home. We had our agenda all in order, including a guided meditation.

The week started as usual, and then, on Tuesday morning, I sat down for meditation. A few moments into my meditation, in full voice, I heard, "I don't want you to do that meditation on Sunday." As if these kinds of voices happen everyday, I responded telepathically, "Why not? It's you?" Because what I recognized from the original communication was that the voice was that of Jesus. I've never heard Jesus' voice before, but I had such a deep inner belief that I had no question who it was. In response to my telepathic message, he replied, "I want you to do something else." In my mind I began pondering, 'Now what do I do?"

Then another voice came through and said, "We want you to channel us." This all happened so quickly there wasn't much time to think, and yet I can remember wondering, 'Huh?' Yet I knew intuitively that this was The Galactic Command. It was as if the information was implanted in my brain. My telepathic response was, 'Does it matter that I've never channeled anybody before in my life?' And they responded in full voice, "Don't worry, we'll take care of that." And then that's all I got, but it was the most astounding, most powerful message I had ever received because it was so clear. And it wasn't something that I could make up from my imagination. It was profoundly clear.

The Celestial Trifecta event began as planned. Surprisingly, there were three to four times more people attending than for most of my events, even though my marketing was the same as always. This in itself indicated something important was up. I knew that "they" had a hand in making that happen.

Many people came for the first time. The activities included energy clearing, setting intentions, purging old experiences in the fire, and drumming with native drums, and yet all of it felt more powerful and more meaningful in ways that we could not describe. Before our meditation, I shared with everyone the messages I had received from Jesus and from Galactic Command. And then when we sat down for meditation, sure enough, they came through with an extremely powerful message, and it was amazing and on-point and necessary for that time frame.

One of my clients, David Graver, has given me permission to share this story. David came to Qigong class and asked me, "Will you tell the ghosts to leave me alone?" I asked, "What do you mean by wanting me to tell the ghosts to leave you alone?" He shared this story:

The night before, David had been reading Life and Teaching of the Masters of the Far East (1924) by Baird Spalding. When he set the book down, he thought, 'I wonder if I should be a Master?' At that moment, a clear bubble about five feet in height appeared in front of him while he had his eyes wide open. Inside the bubble was a hazy figure that looked like a human body taking up the full height of the bubble. This figure spoke to him telepathically, saying, 'You are a good candidate to be a Master, and you should do it.' David was not sure about even having this desire, so he telepathically replied, 'I'm not sure if I want to be a Master.' The figure told him he could when he was ready.

The next topic was that of healing. David had been working on his own digestive healing for the previous couple of days. The figure started working on David's digestive system, and David asked telepathically if he could also work on his eyes. The figure said, 'You can take care of that yourself,' as he continued the work on his digestive system.

He asked the figure its name. The figure said it was George, and that he was new at this. David interpreted that to mean he was a student in the School of Mastery and that he was out practicing his skills, but not as a full Master. The communication ended as quickly as it began, leaving David bewildered and intrigued at what had just happened.

Steps and Methods

While it is not the purpose of meditation OR elevation of consciousness to obtain spiritual gifts, or have other worldly experiences, it is certainly a side benefit. There are so many possibilities, and I have only experienced a small number, partially because I don't focus on them, and partially because, once they show up, they are like any muscle: You have to work at them to get stronger in that area.

Some of the gifts that may come include:

- Clairvoyance or "clear seeing," the ability to see visions with either inner sight or with the physical eyes. It also covers seeing spirits and auras as well. Those who practice mediumship are often clairvoyant (also clairaudient, "clear hearing") so that they can see and speak with those who have passed over. Other clairvoyants may see visions from the past, present, as well as seeing actual future events that have not yet happened on our timeline. They have the ability to transcend the physical dimension where time exists and get information from the eternal moment, where all events occur simultaneously.

- Clairaudience is one of the most handy gifts to have in terms of gathering information, and also surprisingly simple to develop. Imagine being able to hear what spirit guides wanted to tell us. In order to develop clairaudience or "clear hearing," we can try automatic writing or channeling. This develops our inner sense of hearing, allowing us to discern what is our mind chatter and what comes to us from outside our mind. Another way to develop clairaudience is to start talking to our angels, which is what I do all the time. Say things to them and develop a relationship with them. Once we give our permission for them to start talking to us, they start to put words and thoughts into our mind.

- Clairsentience is the ability of "clear sensing." This is quite common for sensitive and intuitive people, and it is the first gift that I realized was available to me and may have been there since childhood, though I was not aware of it. We are least likely to shut down this ability if we have it as a child. This gift is all about sensing things about our surroundings and other people. We can pick up energy about the places we are in, such as homes or workplaces, since buildings, locations, and things give off energy just as people do. We can get a good vibe or feel distinctly uncomfortable in a certain place, or gather information about the past of a place or thing. We can also sense spirits and what the spirits are feeling. When around other people, clairsentients receive clear information about their character and their emotions, as well. It is not easy to fool a clairsentient for this reason, as they can have an uncanny feel for what is going on with another person. Energy doesn't lie, so clairsentient people can often tell a lie when it is spoken by the feel of it, or if the corresponding emotions of the person do not fit what they are saying.

- Claircognizance is the ability to just know something without being aware of how you know it. It is referred to as "clear knowing." At times in our life, information becomes available to us without a vision or without spirit telling us — we simply know! Recently, a friend made a huge shift in her life and took a job with a company, leaving her past work connections out in the cold. When this happened, I knew she would not be with that company very long, and I had no reason to know — I just knew. Within three months, my friend had left the new company and reconnected with those she had left behind. I knew as though I had time traveled and seen it. Claircognizance is not as well known or discussed as the other 'clairs,' yet most of us get that perfect knowledge at times.

Additional gifts that can come as you elevate your level of consciousness include —

- Telepathy — the ability to read people's minds and mentally communicate with others, sometimes over a distance

- Telekinesis — the ability to move objects with their mind

- Mediumship — the ability to communicate with the deceased

- Empathy — the ability to sense the emotions that a person is feeling

- Reality warping — the ability to stop time, or change the outcome of an event

- Animal connection — telepathic communication with animals, plants, and other beings, such as crystals and faeries

Other worldly experiences that have become a part of my regular life, that you can experience, too:

- I routinely see and talk with angels and Masters through my inner vision.

- As my relationship with the Masters has developed, they provide me direct audible messages when they desire a specific outcome.

- Medical intuition occurs where I can see inside my clients, and feel and identify stored emotions they have within, and what to do with it to bring them back to their natural perfect state.

- Astral travel is the ability to "leave" your body and go to other places to experience something without the density of the body being there. You may be able to read something in another place without being there, or see what another person is doing somewhere else while your body is stationary.

- Lucid dreaming is being just awake enough to control where you go in your dream state.

- My ability to manifest whatever I think about has become so strong I have to be cautious about what I desire.

Reaching ultimate connection with Source. Christians call it the Kingdom of God. Buddhists call it Enlightenment. Yogis call it Samadhi. And early scholars called it Cosmic Consciousness.

In any case, ultimate connection with Source references the pure bliss state of consciousness that can be reached through concerted effort and right intention. This is the highest state of peace and pure connection to Source that one can experience, and it is attainable by everyone.

This is the ultimate purpose of our repeated incarnations on this earth — to reach this ultimate state of consciousness, this most elevated frequency, so we can be a force of ultimate love for everyone on this planet. This is what I wish for me, and this is what I wish for you. This is what I wish for our world.

Until then, we can behave as if it is already so, and the world will be impacted in an even greater positive way by each person who does so.

Have you had any other worldly experiences? They are not reserved for the highest spiritual gurus or even for those "born" with gifts. They are available to you and me, and everyone. While these experiences are not what we should seek through our spiritual studies, they are helpful, and useful to activate in serving others.

My wish for you is to open to the pure connection of Oneness with Source. We all have experienced multiple lifetimes on our journey toward this mission. It is why we came this time, and the Universal energy is ripe for this to happen for many. Dive deep into your spiritual practice.

When that pure connection occurs, there are no blurred lines, there is no division.

Duality fades. There is only Oneness.

That is what I want for you.

That is what I want for the world.

Intuitive Breakthrough Strategist

Rochel R Rittgers is the author of the book, Radiate, Change Your Frequency, Change Your Life. She is the founder and CEO of Infinite Living Center of Holistic Experience and the Infinite Living Institute. She has been a featured presenter and MC on radio, television and national and international stages sharing her unique techniques to assist people in achieving greater personal and business success.

Rochel is especially passionate about helping people realize who they really are, so that they can step into their most authentic power.

She enjoys clearing people's inner chaos so that they can experience complete inner freedom, and as an acclaimed medical intuitive she is committed to helping clients release buried pain through a combination of her Signature Intensive Emotional Release Therapy, Medical Qigong, and crystal and sound healing so that they can THRIVE in life and in business.

Rochel really enjoys leading and hosting spiritual retreats, loving on her 4-legged fur babies, and climbing trees.

To book Rochel text 309-269-6989